children in the game

Child Prostitution: Strategies for Recovery

Ross A. MacInnes

Published by Street Teams   Telephone: (403) 228•3390
Suite 210, 1505–17 Avenue S.W.   Fax: (403) 244•5202
Calgary, Alberta T2T 0E2   Toll Free: 1•888•525•7772

The publisher wishes to acknowledge that funds for this edition were provided by the David R. Ashford Fund at the Calgary Foundation.

CREDITS:

Editor: Carol Sheehan / CS Communication Strategies, Calgary, AB
Cover Image: Marnie Burkhart, Jazhart Studios Inc., Calgary, AB
Cover Design: Jeremy Drought, Last Impression Publishing Service, Calgary, AB
Pre-Press Production: Last Impression Publishing Service, Calgary, AB
Printing: D.W. Friesen, Altona, MB

CANADIAN CATALOGUING IN PUBLICATION DATA

MacInnes, Ross A. (Ross Alexander), 1946-
    Children in the game

    Includes bibliographical references.
    ISBN 0-9684386-0-1

    1. Child prostitution--Case studies. 2. Teenage prostitution--
Case studies. 3. Prostitutes--Rehabilitation. 4. Prostitutes--
Services for. I. Title.
HQ306.M32 1998   306.74'5   C98-911044-3

Contents

Acknowledgments

I am unbelievably wealthy, yet I have no money in the bank. The fortune that I have is the people I have known in the past and the people I know at the present.

Although they passed away many years ago, my parents set high standards through their Christian lives and their dedication to helping others. The men and women I worked with in the Police Department displayed courage and compassion, and some I knew gave up their lives for the community. The many who work with children are often the same ones who sacrificed personal affluence to work long and hard to ensure the next generation had the maximum chance of succeeding. All of you have given me riches beyond words.

Children in the Game evolved in a unique fashion. As a police officer, I saw the suffering and sorrow of the children on the streets. I also saw some of their victories and miracles. I recorded their stories—both those which ended tragically and those that ended in triumph—to help other children and the people who love them. To the children I give my love and my gratitude; you taught me so much.

To the incredible staff at *Street Teams*—you constantly amaze me. I have never worked with a finer group of people. You smiled at all my frustrations as this project evolved. To Kathy Ashford, who believed in this book and translated that belief into financial support that enabled it to happen, thank you.

To Johanna Bates, counselor, mentor, advisor, consultant, whip and friend, *you* guided this book through its many stages with skill, understanding and patience. Carol Sheehan, my Editor. Wow—what an assignment you took on! Making sense out of piles of paper, computer disks, voice recordings, photocopies, research data and assorted ramblings. You did a marvelous job. To Jeremy Drought, whose artistic eye and production skill brought the entire book together. I thank you all.

But the one who kept me going through it all, and whose faith never wavered, is Dee—my wife and companion for over thirty years. Without your support I could not have done it. Sweetheart, you are my greatest fortune.

Ross A. MacInnes
Calgary, Alberta, September 1998

1
Introduction to the Game: The War and the Prize

On the streets, a child doesn't remain a child for very long.

IT had been a long day. No matter how much I managed to accomplish, a mountain of files still covered my desk. The Vice Squad had blown the lid off something that had been underground for years and now everywhere we turned, there was new information coming to light. I rearranged the pile a bit and put it over until tomorrow; it was late. For the first time in two weeks I managed to make it home and crawl into bed before midnight.

The phone rang, jarring me awake. Groggy, I scrambled for the bedside lamp, and fumbled for the receiver. It was the Night Shift Commander. "I think you better come down here Ross," he said, "The patrol officers came across something you might be interested in."

I scrawled the address on a pad of paper by the bed; it was just after 4:00 A.M. Glancing back at my still-sleeping wife, I shook my head. This was the third call-out in as many weeks. I wondered what I'd find this time?

I pulled up to the address at the same time as one of my senior detective teams. They too were called out of a warm bed—this time by me! If I had to get up, I wasn't going to be the only one. "Good morning guys...this is what we have so far." I relayed the information that I had received over the phone as I drove downtown.

Apparently, a young girl had escaped from a building and phoned the police. In her phone call, she had said that a number of girls were being held against their will, in a storage room, where they had been repeatedly raped. The responding officers located the site, found the girls, and removed them from the building.

The police arrested a number of men and took them to the Detective Division for questioning. The youngsters had already been taken to the hospital, so there was little for us to do at the scene, other than look around.

What we found was like a scene out of an X-rated film. Dirty mattresses, used condoms, locked doors, half-eaten plates of food: all signs that the girls had been held there for some time. The detectives returned to the office to interview the suspects. I went to the hospital to check on the girls.

I spent the next four hours with them. At first, they were reluctant to tell their story, so I sat patiently in their room until they became comfortable with my presence. As dawn broke, their stories gradually and quietly unfolded. Shocked by what they had to tell me, I later became incredibly angry at the adults of the world who had stooped so low as to repeatedly sexually molest and abuse these children. One girl was only twelve years old!

This was more than assault. It was even more than rape. It was the enslaving of young children for use as sexual objects by adults. I knew that the devastation to the lives of these youngsters was immeasurable—if not unthinkable.

• • •

After a lifetime working the streets as a cop in a major city, I still had trouble coming to grips with the absolutely sick individuals who prey on vulnerable children. What I saw during those early morning hours made me question my sanity in taking the position as head of the Vice Squad. Maybe I should have kept the desk job. At least that way I wouldn't be exposed to this garbage—and I could sleep at night.

Maybe not!

As the head of Vice, I worked with my team to re-dedicate the squad's efforts to uncovering and destroying exactly this type of horrific exploitation. Restructuring the squad's mandate didn't take place overnight.

Before taking the job as head of Vice, I'd never worked in an undercover unit. I had no idea of what a detective did, nor what it would be like to wear civilian clothes to work. What I did know was how to sort out priorities, and how to work with people.

For the first six months in my new posting, I kept my mouth shut. I rode with the teams assigned to investigate pimps. I sat around in smoke-filled strip joints, visited massage parlors, and talked with the women in the escort business. I even put on old clothes and worked undercover stings on the street. I read every piece of literature I could find on the whole issue of prostitution—examining its history, dynamics, and evolution, and the political issues it generated. I looked at the Vice Squad's mandate, conducted extensive meetings with the members of my unit, and gradually began to understand what was going on around me.

Considering data from my study, the unit's investigations, and the changes within society, we decided to focus the Squad's attention upon the crime of children being sexually exploited for money by adults. Soon after we developed this mission, we identified the target, dedicated ourselves to the vision, and obtained sufficient staff to begin our operations.

What we didn't have were the victims. We knew they were out there but every effort we made to uncover this deeply hidden activity met with dead-ends, operational disasters, and frustration. All I could do was encourage the men and women of the squad to keep trying.

• • •

One night in late autumn, two of my experienced detectives were cruising the "high track" stroll. This was an area adjacent to the downtown core where the more attractive prostitutes plied their trade.

There has always existed an understanding between the working girls and the police about where the stroll's boundaries were and the expected codes of conduct. The police required the prostitutes to carry identification at all times. The detectives monitored the area, cruising the streets and avenues for several blocks in all directions surrounding the high track stroll. They made some routine checks, ensuring that the prostitutes had observed the informal street rules. They also checked for strays who had wandered off, new girls attempting to increase the boundaries, or anyone deciding to strike off in new directions.

As the two officers rounded a corner, they took note of the fact that there were two new girls working the sidewalk several blocks from the main area. They decided to have a word with them.

They asked the girls to have a seat in the car, and started their questioning. The investigators had never seen these youngsters before, and the questions they posed did not elicit the normal responses. The stories the girls offered were full of holes. They carried no identification, and their style of dress didn't fit with the generally enticing, exotic clothing of the girls working several blocks away. As the detectives continued the interview, the account the girls gave began to fall apart. Finally, the two officers took them back to the Vice Squad office and conducted a more in-depth interrogation.

At the squad office, the children's tale began to unfold. Though interviewed separately, the girls' stories were remarkably similar. Both provided details describing what we now call "trick pads." The absolute horror of the girls' account rocked even the two seasoned veterans. Both children, one aged thirteen and the other fourteen, related how men kept them in various locations with their every move monitored by a "minder," a person assigned to feed, clothe, and keep them in line. Using the girls' fragmented accounts, the detectives pieced together a devastating scenario.

When their pimp lined up a base of clients, he would transport the girls to a specified location, and turn the girls over to a group of men for the sole purpose of satisfying their sexual appetites. One of the girls described how she had been put in a small room with only a mattress and a box of condoms. For the next sixteen hours, she lay there, servicing one customer after another. In total, forty-two men had intercourse with this child during that one night. The second girl corroborated the story, and the narration of her experiences was even more shocking. She was raped anally so many times that she now had to wear adult diapers because her sphincter muscles were damaged to the point where she no longer had control over her bowels.

• • •

At last we had our first real break. I immediately authorized the team to work as much overtime as they needed and to call in whatever additional resources or staff they felt were necessary.

The entire unit mobilized and the department assigned additional investigators to the squad. The children's truly horrifying story, together with their evidence, permitted us to lay initial charges. We didn't feel, however, that our grasp of the activity was complete. In a conference with my commander, I discussed the status of the investigation and the methods we could use to extend the scope of inquiry.

With his endorsement, I compiled a press release and distributed it to every news outlet in the city. The response was overwhelming. Concerned parents, who had kept their fears secret, phoned and expressed their support. The general public became enraged; when they read and heard the various news reports, they demanded action. Unsure how or where to direct their anger, they knew only that they wanted to do something. From the tips, leads and general information that poured in, we increased our knowledge substantially about the city's child prostitution industry. Investigations uncovered more sex-trade rings, and the police arrested more pimps and brought them before the courts. The impact of a few press releases unleashed far-reaching consequences; at the same time, data for our already burgeoning files poured into the office.

As the number of young girls who were identified and "brought out of the life" increased, the load on various social agencies also escalated. We made a conscious decision not to charge the girls with any criminal offenses, but rather to treat them as victims in this whole mess. This approach meant we could not call into play the normal processes involving Juvenile Detention and other lockup facilities.

Some of the victims we contacted had run away from good homes and could eventually return home. The majority of the girls, however, were either permanent wards of the government or from disconnected and dysfunctional families who could not—or would not—take the children back. The load on child care workers became increasingly heavy. We had failed to take into account both the uniqueness of these children and the nature of their victimization. We faced a blunt reality: the system had a distinct lack of knowledge about how to deal with these children.

I interviewed many girls. I made notes on their stories, their struggles, their fears. I saw their scars, and watched them as their eyes became clouded with memories of dark places and terrifying events.

For the most part, their backgrounds reflected years of physical, sexual, and emotional abuse. Street life became an attractive alternative for them. Most had no idea of what snares they were falling into until it became too late to back away from the predators who trapped them into prostitution. They became nocturnal creatures, living for the night, sleeping during the day. Many had been out of school for several years by this time and, as a consequence, were trailing behind their peers.

Additionally, the girls' values had been transformed, along with their sense of self-worth—and even their language. Soon it became abundantly clear that if we were to affect any type of long-term change in the lives of these children, we would first have to educate those on the front lines.

Child care workers, school guidance counselors, clinicians, juvenile probation officers, and others who worked directly with this group would have to increase their knowledge about the phenomenon of child prostitution. The Vice Squad designed and initiated a program, and presented it through a day-long seminar entitled *High Heels & Teddy Bears*. After we sent notices to all of the concerned agencies, the registrations received filled the seminar to capacity. Dozens of names remained on a waiting list.

We produced a special dictionary of street terms that has since been expanded and is included at the back of this book. Vice Squad detectives made presentations covering topics such as how pimps recruit and control the girls, the nature of "the game," and the difficulty in gaining successful convictions against the predators.

Two girls joined the detectives. Former prostitutes, they had made it out of "the life" and came to tell their stories. The participants spent hours listening to the presentations and asked hundreds of questions.

The impact we began to see on the community was both quick in its coming and gratifying in its intensity. The extensive coverage given to the issue began spreading to newspapers and magazines beyond the local area. Other countries began to pick up on the story, and requests for more information began to pour in to our offices. The issue began to hit home in many communities throughout North America—and the judicial system began to take notice.

Where the investigators once had problems meeting with prosecutors, they now found themselves being invited to address legal conferences. Judges who had shunned these cases were volunteering to hear them in court. Eighteen months earlier, officers of the court found difficulty in securing a pimping conviction that would garner anything more than two years in jail. Now we were seeing ten year sentences being handed down to pimps who marketed the services of children.

More women in their twenties and thirties who had once been prostitutes and had "squared up," began to step forward. They too wanted to contribute in some meaningful way and we welcomed their assistance and their knowledge. Later, committees concerned about the proper delivery of social services to young girls asked some of the women to join them. Some served on other committees, aiding in the design of educational opportunities.

Business organizations asked for more information, and their ability to raise money benefited agencies who had previously struggled for even meager funds. Professional groups offered to assist with job-training and placement; community associations and service groups also began exploring ways in which to help.

Almost immediately, I was inundated with requests to undertake speaking engagements, appear on talk shows, respond to inquiries, and give advice and information to a variety of groups. Four or five external engagements a week quickly became the norm. Teachers, counselors, child care workers, and concerned parents wanted more and more information.

At many of my speaking venues, the audience members asked questions: about the background of girls who became involved; how pimps recruited them; why the girls just didn't leave when they found themselves in too deep; and what happened to them after they got out of the life. I recounted stories about the girls, answering their questions by describing the youngsters' slide into child prostitution, and the oppressive life they led. At all of these talks, the dictionary of street terminology, compiled by one of the detectives in the squad, became a much sought-after document.

I maintained constant contact with many of the youngsters; a number of them were on the way out of prostitution and recovering from their ordeals. Occasionally, I would take one of these girls with me and their earnest tales hit home as nothing else could! To see girls, some as young as eleven, relate years of abuse at the hands of adults brought tears to the eyes of even the most cynical.

I honored as many speaking engagements as I could but as the requests grew, I knew I needed a different method of delivering this information.

Some of the girls' stories were transcribed and I distributed them in printed form at various forums. As the variety of stories increased, it became clear to me that there was a necessity to compile them into a book. *Children in the Game* presents some of the stories of these girls. Some of these stories became the core content of an award winning video, *The Butterfly Collectors*.

Children in the Game does not sensationalize these stories. A straightforward recounting of them is sensational enough. Rather, the stories serve as case studies—illustrations to help describe the devastating reality of children trapped in prostitution. This book is more than a social documentary about the horror of a vast, growing population of children sexually abused by adults.

The first part of *Children in the Game* focuses on the lives of five child prostitutes, from their "initiation" to the street through to the conclusion of their time in "the life." Using frank, anecdotal descriptions, I orient each case with the girl's background, explaining that though the origins vary, each story unfolds to follow an insidious pattern of entrapment and exploitation.

In every case study, you will witness a young girl pass from one encounter to another in a continual downward spiral of fear and degradation. You will understand how her loss of self-esteem and her surrender of personal power results in abuse, damage, and hopelessness. Each story is substantially true, though some details have been altered to protect individual children and to safeguard evidence still before the courts.

The purpose behind telling the stories of Tanya, Kara, Jackie, Sukan, and Christine is not to sensationalize, titillate, or to horrify—it is to educate and to begin answering the essential question I hope all readers will ask themselves: *"What can I do?"*

The second part of *Children in the Game* summarizes what we know about child prostitution and guides us to an action plan. The "players" come to life in these chapters. The pimps and the girls they exploit are placed within a cultural context. Learning the methods of recruitment, the systematized exploitation, violence, and destruction employed by the pimps teaches us to identify the enemy in this cult-like enterprise. Knowing their language, predicting their strategies, and understanding the victims of their "game" is key to reclaiming our children from the night.

At the back of this book is a glossary of street terminology—a small dictionary of terms that I call "street talk." By reading this section, readers gain some insight into the harsh realities of this subculture—for language carries the logic and ethos of a culture.

By recognizing that recovery from the street is not necessarily recovery of the child prostitute's future, *Children in the Game* goes on to map the process of restoring a damaged child to safety. New players enter her world. They are a team of specialists that she learns to trust—to repair, accept, assist, guide, inspire, protect and teach—as she slowly gains mastery of her life. Though they recognize that her life has forever changed, the team believes it is a life that will see health and hope restored.

Children in the Game describes the team concept and illustrates how a team operates. After earning a child prostitute's trust, the team is there to help her when she decides to leave the sexual slavery of the streets. After guiding her through this "intervention process," the team does not disband or dissolve. The majority of their work lies ahead as they continue to support, protect, and guide the child through the "recovery process."

Children in the Game is a handbook for battle, designed for use by every adult who honors, values and wishes to protect children. It targets our enemy and equips us with the weapons for the fight by providing insights into a subculture that sexually exploits and destroys children. Armed with knowledge about how this culture thrives, we can, through time-tested and proven methods for intervention and recovery, begin the process of healing and restoration. It's a long process, a difficult battle, but the prize— our children—is worth winning.

2
Tanya

I've failed at school. I've failed to keep my mom and dad together. I've failed to stay in a group home. I've failed on three suicide attempts. I've failed in the drug treatment program. I've failed to make enough money for my man. I'm a failure.

S HE stood shivering. The street lights above formed swirling tunnels as they pushed their glow through the blowing snow. The sound of the wind, moaning through the gaps between the empty office towers, mirrored her state of mind. The occupants of the few cars still traveling Third Avenue passed by with barely a glance at the little girl determinedly holding her place on the street. Her feet, encased in cheap plastic boots, had lost all feeling hours ago. With her little fists tucked inside her short leather jacket, she made a vain effort to keep them from freezing as well. The skirt, barely covering her upper thighs, had long since lost any illusion of warmth. The bitter cold served only to remind her of the day itself—her birthday. Today she turned thirteen.

It was an important day. She was now a teenager and, since turning her first trick a few hours earlier, she was now a whore. She sobbed quietly, the tears freezing quickly on her rouged cheeks. She was so sad. So tired. So cold. So lonely.

She looked up as a blue van turned onto Third Avenue from the cross street. Moving to the edge of the sidewalk she leaned forward and looked directly into the face of the driver. "Giving him the eye" as she'd been instructed, was the first contact she made with potential customers; it was also the signal to clients that she was working the street. The man looked back and pulled to the curb a few feet past her spot. She hurried over to the door of the van, swung it open, and climbed onto the seat.

Maybe it was the cold. Perhaps it was the desperate need "to break" just one more time in order to avoid a beating by Drew. Whatever the reason, she didn't follow street rules in sizing up her date. She neglected to check under the seat and in the glove box for portable radios that would have told her she was negotiating with a vice officer. She neglected to check the license number against the bad date sheet, a list of dangerous "johns," given to her earlier by a front line street agency. She didn't check the back of the van for other passengers, nor did she do the cop check that should be standard action in haggling over the act and amount. She only welcomed the warmth of the van and the chance for human contact.

The van moved into the developing storm.

Anyone passing would have quickly formed an opinion. This was just another street prostitute—a woman earning a living through the sale of sexual services. Had they looked at her face and clothes they may have concluded that she was over eighteen. She was doing what she did because she made her own decision to enter the life—walk the walk and talk the talk. Yes, they would have thought to themselves, "She sure must be chilly wearing such skimpy clothes, but if she didn't want to be out there, why didn't she leave?"

As they passed, they may have commented about the decrease in property values since the hookers moved in. They might even have engaged in some light philosophical discussions about the need for a red light district. Maybe they would have rationalized about the oft-quoted axiom, "You can't get rid of it, so tax it and we can all make money." They might have chuckled about the time they drove around throwing pennies at the girls, blowing their car horns and yelling obscene insults. "After all, they're just hookers aren't they?"

• • •

No, Tanya was not "just a hooker"—she was also a little girl. A small child who once dreamed big dreams. Dreams of growing up. Dreams of dancing with the cute guy in her English class. Dreams of being a nurse, of marrying the most handsome man in the world. Of living in exotic places, of traveling to foreign countries, of being popular, being pretty.

A little girl's dreams.

Her real name was Elizabeth. She was called "Becky" by her grandmother, "Beth" by her teachers, "Liza" by her mother, and "Muffin" by her father. Her street name is "Tanya."

• • •

Elizabeth had grown up in what many consider a normal family. Her mother and father were still married, both had reasonably good jobs, and the family never missed a meal or a mortgage payment. The children spent summers at camps or traveling to the lake where they had a cottage. Two older brothers were attending university and both were doing well. Although the evenings were silent around the house, there was little to indicate to various friends and neighbors that this was not an average middle class family.

She was twelve when the problems first appeared. Momentary bouts of defiance and anger at home usually related to topics about responsibility, acting her age, or her new circle of friends. Each new conflict grew more difficult to resolve than the one before. Her mother tried to be understanding but couldn't seem to come to grips with Elizabeth's new found independence. What would start off as a mother-daughter talk always resulted in a screaming match. Both Elizabeth and her mother would end up calling each other names and hurting each other deeply. Neither wanted it this way but both seemed powerless to stop the escalating tension.

As the situation at home deteriorated, her father attempted to right the situation. His method was to use discipline, such as a grounding or loss of phone privileges, or her allowance, in an attempt to "teach her responsibility." These approaches, like the mother-daughter chats, served only to drive them further apart.

Intervention by a family therapist had some positive results but, from Elizabeth's point of view, the adults seemed to make it out to be all her fault.

School became a drag. All the studying, boring teachers, and criticism about her small circle of friends from the "bad crowd" piled one frustration on top of another. Things had to change. Without consulting Elizabeth, her parents decided that a change in schools would be the answer. And so, they made the change. Now she not only had the same frustrations, she'd also lost her small circle of friends.

Gradually, Elizabeth began hanging around the food court at the mall. She could smoke in the area and there were always people around who would give her a few dollars, share some "butts," and in general, be the friends she always wanted.

She was sitting alone at a table one day when she heard the pleasant voice of a man standing next to her.

"May I sit down?" he asked.

She silently pointed to the empty chair across from her.

He sat down and pushed a plate of fries and gravy to the center of the table.

"Help yourself, I can't eat them all," he said with smile as he gestured to the plate.

Elizabeth slowly picked up one and put it in her mouth.

"Having problems at home?" he asked.

She nodded.

"Look at me," he commanded in a quiet voice.

Elizabeth lifted her head and met his eyes.

For the next hour Andrew spoke to Elizabeth. He was so understanding, so kind, so thoughtful. He seemed to know exactly what she was going through and the turmoil inside her. He instinctively knew she wanted more from life than what she had: nice things, a safe place to call home, and people around her who could understand her and respect her. Her new found friend seemed to be the only person she had ever met who truly cared about her.

As she rose to leave, he took her by the hand and walked her the length of the shopping plaza. They joked and laughed as they walked. Never had Elizabeth had so much attention, been so comfortable or felt so safe. She felt herself falling in love.

Lightly grasping her elbow, he steered her into a boutique. Racks of leather jackets lined the walls. Blouses, slacks, and fancy sweaters hung in fascinating displays on racks on the sales floor.

Andrew selected a particularly striking black leather jacket and slipped it over her shoulders.

"Do you like this one?" he asked with a smile.

"It's beautiful," gasped Elizabeth. "I've never seen anything so lovely."

"It's yours; just let me pay for it," he said as he moved to the sales counter.

Before Elizabeth could protest, he pulled a large roll of bills from his pocket and swiftly counted out the required amount.

After returning with Andrew to the food court, Elizabeth had thanked him as best she could and tentatively started to leave. With a wave and a smile, he let her go. They promised to meet again the following day at the same spot.

Walking home, Elizabeth could only marvel at her good fortune. Imagine, an older man thinking she was beautiful! Not only that, he'd actually bought her a present. She fingered the soft leather thoughtfully. As the texture of the jacket moved between her fingers, she thought back over the last year, to the number of times people ridiculed her, the fights, the tears, the therapists who said they cared but couldn't be bothered to return her phone calls. Her face clouded in anger as she thought about school.

Her grades had fallen steadily since she transferred to the new school. She lost count thinking over the number of times she had been sent to the principal's office. She thought of the saccharine sweetness of the Guidance Counselor and all that phony caring expressed by her home room teacher.

Tears trickled their way down her cheeks as she walked up the steps and opened the door to the house. As usual, no one was home.

Over the next week she met Andrew with increasing frequency. He bought her cigarettes, meals and clothes. One day he even bought her a cute necklace. Although he was ten years older than Elizabeth, the difference didn't seem to matter. He treated her with respect—and really listened to her. Soon she was madly, hopelessly in love.

Late Saturday afternoon, sitting once again at what she had come to think of as "their" table, she longed to see him and to share her latest agony. That morning her own father called her a *slut*. Sure, she put on some make up. Yes, she wore tight jeans and a blouse cut lower than her other ones. But she wanted to wear these things. After all, Andrew bought them for her and she wanted to look good. She didn't care if she ever saw her mother and "dad" again. If they called her a slut, maybe she was. Her thoughts were interrupted as a small wrapped box was placed in front of her.

She looked up and smiled. It was Andrew.

She glanced down at the box.

"For me?" she asked with a child's infectious anticipation.

"Yup, for you," he replied, sliding into the opposite seat.

Eagerly she tore off the wrapping. It was a small crystal figurine of a unicorn. She giggled delightedly.

"I've always wanted one of these," she gasped. "Why did you get it for me?"

"Because I care about you, that's why," he replied. "Do you really like it?"

"I love it!" she answered. "It's been a shitty day, but this makes up for it."

"Tell me about your shitty day," he grinned.

Elizabeth recounted in detail the latest fights at home. He listened attentively, a speculative look entering his eyes.

"I have a place where you can stay," he mentioned casually. "There are a couple of other girls there too. We kinda look out for one another."

"Could I stay there too?" she asked tentatively. She'd been disappointed so often in her young life; she couldn't quite believe that anyone would offer to help her.

"You certainly can," he replied rising to his feet. "Let's head over there now and wake them up."

A fleeting thought passed through Elizabeth's mind as to why the girls were just getting up in the middle of the afternoon, but the assurance with which Andrew moved set her fears aside and she hurried to catch up to him.

They left the shopping center and headed for the car. She'd never seen his vehicle, although he did tell her it was a sports car. She was astonished when he took the key from his pocket and opened the door of a shiny red Corvette.

"Hop in," he said as he swung open the door.

Elizabeth happily rode the short distance to Andrew's apartment. When she arrived she was introduced to two young girls who were watching television. Karen and Angel barely glanced at Andrew and the new arrival.

The apartment was sparsely furnished, with an old sofa and a TV in the living room, a small kitchen with the basic appliances, and a bedroom with two mattresses on the floor. Clothes, empty beer cans, overflowing ashtrays, and remnants of take-out food containers littered the rooms. The stale odors of past parties and unwashed clothes hung in the air. Elizabeth shuddered involuntarily, but the feeling quickly passed—at least here she felt safe.

During the course of the next few hours she gradually got to know her new roommates. They seemed to speak a foreign language. References to "dates," "turning out," "trap," and "bumping" punctuated their conversation. Confused at first, Elizabeth gradually realized they were speaking about prostitution. "Dates" were liaisons with various men. "Turning out" was a reference to being put on the street, while "trap" referred to the money they turned over to someone at the end of their evenings. When it came to "bumping," Elizabeth realized they were speaking about her, and that they intended to "bump" or recruit her for Andrew—or "Drew"—as she learned he preferred.

The discussion held both a revulsion and a fascination to her. She'd known about "the life" but had never met anyone involved in it. As their conversations progressed, she became aware that they were trying to pressure her into working the street as a prostitute. She adamantly refused to even consider it.

Elizabeth couldn't believe their suggestions; she only wanted to talk to Andrew and to clear up this obvious misunderstanding. Andrew, however, had left some time earlier, "to take care of business."

At about 9:00 P.M. he returned. By that time the other girls had dressed in "Ho clothes": short skirts, up-lift bras, high heels and spectacular make up. Andrew barely glanced at Elizabeth as he shepherded the girls out into the hallway.

With a brief, "We'll talk later," he closed the door.

In the half-hour that he was gone, Elizabeth realized that she was envious of the attention he had paid to the others and resentful that he had left her behind. Wasn't she pretty enough? Not sexy enough? Didn't he care about her? All her insecurities came flooding back.

When he did return, she greeted him warmly, throwing her arms around him and kissing him full on the mouth. She was delighted when he returned her affections, and as he scooped her up in his arms and took her to the bedroom, she didn't resist; in fact she welcomed it.

Their lovemaking was gentle, yet persistent. She had never made love before, and when he softly instructed her in what to do, she eagerly responded. As they lay together in the aftermath, she chided him for not taking her with the other girls.

"You're not a *whore*," he replied. "You're special! I have great things in mind for you and me."

Curled in his strong arms she felt as if she belonged. He spoke of their future together: the trips, the cars, the holidays. She felt proud when he told her she would be his "main" and together they would run the other girls. Now she was getting the respect she deserved!

He cautioned her about talking to the other girls. There was no need for them to know about their secret arrangement, he explained. They would be jealous of the attention he paid to her.

Several times that evening and night, he left her for brief periods of time. Each time he returned, he pulled from his pocket a growing wad of bills. He counted out fives, tens, twenties, and even a fifty and placed the money in a locked safe under the bed.

Just after 2:00 A.M., he came back with both girls. He also had some clothes for her and instructed her to dress for a party. She slipped into high heels, a shiny black mini skirt and low-cut blouse. She put on make up and some jewelry she found on a shelf in the bedroom. When she emerged she was flattered by Drew's critical eye. She made some minor adjustments under his direction, and all four of them left the apartment.

Riding downtown, she became mildly upset when he didn't choose her to ride in the front with him. She and Karen sat in the back while Drew and Angel discussed the business of the night.

They pulled into a parking lot on the still brightly lit strip. She noted the long lineup at the entrance and was proud when a man waved Andrew along with his girls to the front of the line and into the noisy bar. She had snuck into one or two bars before—but never to such a lively one. The flashing lights above the dance floor, the smell of pot in the air, and the babble of voices all added to her feeling of being grown-up and worldly.

Andrew introduced her to a number of men. She noted that almost all were black, as was Drew, but the majority of the girls were white. Marijuana, whisky, beer—in fact anything you wanted was there for the asking. She smoked a little dope, drank half a bottle of beer and marveled at her good fortune in being invited into such an exciting world. There was no way she was going back now!

By 4:00 A.M. she was in heaven. The effects of the alcohol and drugs had given her a feeling of euphoria. When Andrew suddenly took her arm and walked out to the car with the other girls in tow, she was anxious for the next adventure.

Slipping quickly behind the wheel, he said, "We're leaving town," and without so much as a glance at the others, started the car.

As they left the city lights and entered the blackness of the countryside she felt nervous in the shadow of his silence. Angel, still in the front seat, questioned him. Without a moment's hesitation, he backhanded her across the face. She started to cry.

"I'm sorry babe, it's just that bitch Lacy signed on me today," he said softly. "I lost my temper. Forgive me?"

Still stunned by the stinging blow, Angel forced a smile. "Of course I do, I know how pissed off you are—but don't take it out on me. I'll never sign."

Elizabeth whispered to Karen, "What's he mean by *sign*?"

Karen leaned over and said softly, "Lacy went to the police and charged Andrew with *Living on the Avails*."

She looked meaningfully into Elizabeth's eyes, but elaborated no further. Turning her shoulder to the window, Karen settled down in the seat to sleep.

Elizabeth drifted off to sleep as well and woke when they stopped at the first traffic light in a city she didn't recognize. Andrew continued into the downtown core, made a few turns and pulled into the rear of a ramshackle duplex.

Everyone got out, stretched and walked up the steps. Drew knocked on the door and a girl—wearing a rumpled man's shirt and nothing else—opened it.

"Hi honey, why didn't you call?" she asked.

"I didn't have time," he replied curtly.

Andrew briefly explained that Lacy had signed on him and that he wanted to be out of town for a while until things got straightened out. The girl cursed and muttered a few threats of what should happen to Lacy, then waved the other girls into the front room.

He introduced Elizabeth as "one of the new girls," and she was shown a place to sleep. It was just an old fold out bed, but she was so tired she was asleep in an instant. The murmur of voices in the other room became a backdrop to her exhausted slumber. A few snatches of conversation worked their way into her mind. Something about "working," "turning out" and "respect" was mentioned, but it made no impact on her. She would sort it out later.

She woke just after noon. Andrew and the girl who had opened the door were gone. She was alone with Angel and Karen. As she searched through the fridge for something to eat, the conversation revolved around her, and they raised the question about her "working" like the rest of them.

She refused once again. This time, however, they didn't let the subject drop. When she attempted to phone her family, "to let them know where she was," the telephone was roughly snatched from her hand and both girls physically attacked her. They stopped only when she quit fighting back and lay huddled in a corner.

"Wait 'til Drew gets back. He gets real mad if you don't show him respect. If I were you, I'd do anything he asks," Karen said with a menacing grin, "otherwise he'll tune you up like you deserve."

Gradually Elizabeth composed herself and they dropped the subject of turning tricks. The other girls chatted about clothes, Drew, bad dates, and how they looked. Not once did they draw Elizabeth into the conversation.

It was early evening when he returned. He was in an ugly mood and the girls avoided him. As he threw things around the small kitchen, cursing everyone and everything, his focus rested on Elizabeth.

"Come here," he ordered, the anger in his voice vanishing instantly.

She moved slowly towards him. He put his arm around her and set her on his lap.

"I'm in trouble. Some guys I owe money to are threatening to kill me. I need money in a hurry. Can you help me just this once?" he questioned, eyes searching her face, pleading.

"I don't have any money, Andrew," she replied, "...otherwise I'd be glad to help you out."

He looked at her for a few moments. He set her back on her feet, moved her back a pace or two and speculatively appraised her up and down.

"Will you do some work for me just this once?" he asked, looking up into her eyes.

"You mean...?" Elizabeth trembled. She couldn't bring herself to say the word.

"Yes," Drew replied softly. "I want you to help me out tonight. The other girls will look out for you. It's just this once. Just until I get out of the jam I'm in. After all, I helped you out when you were broke and in trouble—now you owe me something."

Elizabeth hesitated. She didn't want to do it, but she did owe him a big debt. Besides, it was only going to be "just this once."

"O.K., but you've got to promise me it's only tonight," she said.

"I give you my word," he replied. "After all, you're very special to me...and if I wasn't in this shit, I wouldn't even think about it. The other girls will tell you what to do."

Having said that, he stood up and once again left the apartment.

As if on cue, Angel and Karen entered the room.

"So, Drew's turning you out tonight is he?" Angel laughed. "Well, let's get a few things straight. First, we look out for each other. Nobody down there gives a shit about you, so we look after one another. That means you look out for us and we look out for you. You don't talk to anybody except us and the dates. You don't talk to another girl, nor another girl's man. If you do, you're in big shit."

For the next few minutes Angel explained how things worked on the street. Drew wouldn't be down on "the drag" to pick up the money. The girl, whose house they were staying in, would come by regularly to pick it up. Tisha, as she was called, was Drew's "wifey" or "main" and would be the only one to contact the girls on the street. When Elizabeth asked why, the other girls giggled.

"So you can't sign on him, stupid," Karen replied. "Didn't you notice that he never told you what to do, just to 'help him out'? He's real smart about that sort of thing."

Both girls then sat down at the table with Elizabeth. They described how to "give the look" when cars drove by. They explained that it was $50 for a hand job, $70 for a blow, $80 for a straight lay, and $100 for a half and half. They told her how to dress, how to do the "cop check" to determine if the date was an undercover officer, and how to handle a rough date that started to get physical with her. They explained that she was expected to "break" or accept dates, do the job, and return to her spot as quickly as she could.

For a few minutes, their conversation sparked with a rapid fire list of street names that Elizabeth could use. Elizabeth eagerly accepted the camaraderie, tossing in several names herself. They rejected most of the names because they were already taken, but when she suggested "Tanya," everyone agreed that it was a nice short name and sounded sexy. From now on everyone, except Drew and the other girls, would know her as Tanya. For the rest of her street life, the name would stick. To the street world, "Elizabeth" was dead.

At 11:00 P.M. they called a cab. When it arrived, the three girls rode to the drag and got out at an intersection. For the first half hour they stood together. Angel was the first "to break," getting a date with a middle-aged man driving a small import car. Tanya watched as Angel sat in the car for a few minutes getting to know the john as well as she could.

"Getting a feel for him," was the way she had earlier described this activity. "You have to go with your gut. If you have a bad feeling, get out of the car right away. You can't be too picky or you won't get any dates, but you have to protect yourself too."

A number of cars were circling the block. As each one passed, Tanya became bolder, bending down to look directly at the driver, smiling and moving closer to the curb. Several marked patrol cars passed and she waved brightly to the officers. A number of them smiled and waved back, obviously flattered by her attention. Not one thought to stop and check her age or I.D.

By midnight she thought that her night was going to pass uneventfully and she worried about what Drew would say if she didn't bring back enough money to help him out. Just as she had these concerns, a car pulled up a few feet past her. As she'd done on several occasions, she moved to the passenger side and opened the door.

The driver was a younger man, probably in his mid-twenties, neatly dressed and wearing a beaming smile.

"Are you working?" he asked.

"Depends on what you're looking for," Tanya replied. She remembered the girls' warning about making the initial offer, because she could be busted if it was an undercover cop.

They bantered back and forth, and after the customer had named an act, they settled on the amount and drove off.

It seemed so easy, Tanya reflected, when she returned fifteen minutes later. She had $70 tucked inside her blouse and felt good that she would now be able to help Andrew out of the jam he was in.

As she stepped back onto the curb, Tisha drove up in Drew's car. "How did it go?" she asked.

"Not too bad at all," Tanya replied. "In fact it was easier than I thought."

"I thought you'd like it," Tisha said. "Now give me the trap."

"The what?" Tanya asked.

"The trap—the money," Tisha replied. "Give me the $70 you charged him. It was seventy wasn't it? It better be!"

"Yes, it was seventy," Tanya said as she reached inside her blouse. "Here it is."

She handed the money over to Tisha and, when she left, Tanya once again took up her position on the street.

By 3:00 A.M. she had only turned the one trick. The weather had deteriorated and, when she asked the other girls about going home, they laughed. "You'll have to do better than one date if you want any respect," Angel said.

The same cab that had taken them to the drag several hours earlier returned. Angel and Karen both hopped in the taxi and Tanya followed. She settled back in the seat with a relieved sigh.

"Are we going home now?" she asked no one in particular.

"Never," replied Karen. "We're going to the club. You'll have to stay here and work a while longer. Drew will be down to pick you up." Slowly, Tanya opened the door and got back out of the taxi.

Tanya felt scared as she stepped from the warmth of the cab onto the street. She knew that the $70 she had turned earlier wasn't enough, but hadn't Drew promised her it was only this once? She didn't really mind having to work a few more hours but, as she looked up and down the street, she realized that not only had Drew's girls left, so had all the others. She was alone! Thirteen years old and totally alone.

• • •

Maybe it was something just that simple that caused her to throw caution to the wind and jump into a van with a total stranger: the need to be wanted by somebody. Anybody.

As she held her hands over the defroster, she took a closer look at the driver. He was middle-aged—about forty-five, she guessed—with a receding hairline. He wore old but clean work clothes and a light jacket. She could barely make out his features in the dim glow of the dashboard lights. He looked over at her.

"So, how much ya charge?" he inquired.

"It depends on what you want," Tanya replied. She was gaining her composure again and tried to remember all the instructions the other girls had given her. She recalled one in which both parties had to agree to the act and amount before you left in a john's car. Oh well, she thought, I'm out of the cold at least.

"Just a lay," the man replied. "I don't have a place, so we'll have to do it in the van. I know a place on the outskirts."

"Well then that will be $80. You'll have to wear a condom though."

"Okay...eighty bucks. What's your name?"

"Tanya."

"Well Tanya, you looked pretty cold out there. Not many girls working this time of night, especially with the weather and all. I didn't see a soul out there." He moved the van away from the curb. Snow swirled in the headlights.

Tanya began to feel a bit uncomfortable. She wished now she had taken some precautions before she got into the van.

"No, there were a few still out there," she lied. "My girlfriends were just up the street. I saw them when we drove by."

The man was quiet as he drove. Tanya began to worry that he had seen through her lie and that he would be rough on her. She'd been warned about bad dates, but she had been so cold!

The city blocks passed. Tanya attempted to start a conversation a number of times but he remained unresponsive to her overtures and they spent the remainder of the drive in silence. The storm outside had intensified and the wind picked up as they left the city limits behind. The blackness beyond the headlights served only to bring home to Tanya how fully she was under his control. She couldn't jump from the van at this speed and, mile by mile, she was beginning to feel increasingly afraid.

The van slowed and, with a quick twist of the wheel, turned onto a gravel road. The driver continued driving slowly. Tanya reached for the door handle. Even if she froze, she thought, it was better than staying with this man.

As she opened the door to jump, he reached over and grasped her arm.

"Where do you think you're going?" he yelled. "I agreed to the amount, you bitch, and I'm going to get my piece!"

He slammed on the brakes and the van skidded to a halt on the edge of the road. With a quick motion and without letting go of her arm, he slid into the rear of the van, dragging Tanya with him. He grasped her shoulders and forced her down on the plywood covered floor of the vehicle. With a vicious blow from a closed fist, he hit her in the face. Tanya struggled, and as he repeatedly smashed her head against the floor, she cried a little girl's cry.

Several miles away, a lone police officer was completing his patrol. It had been relatively uneventful thus far—a few minor accidents, a car stuck in the drifts—just a routine shift on a stormy night. He headed back towards the station.

He turned the heater up and, looking out the front window, thought how bad the storm was getting. It sure would be a relief to park the cruiser and book off. It was late and his wife wouldn't be up, but he thought he might make a hot cup of tea before he turned in for the night. He smiled ruefully and shook his head as a van pulled from a side road onto the highway. What anyone would be doing out, driving around at this time of night, was anyone's guess. He reached down for the toggle switch and activated the overhead lights. The van pulled to the side of the road.

He noted the license plates and radioed the number in to the dispatcher. Picking his fur cap from the seat beside him, and grasping a flashlight, he walked to the driver's side of the van.

"Good evening sir, where are you headed?" he asked.

"Just heading for town. I took a wrong turn trying to find my sister's place and got mixed up in the storm. Is anything wrong?"

"No, nothing's wrong, could I see your driver's license, registration, and insurance, please?"

As the man dug through his wallet for the documents, the officer took a few moments to flash his light into the interior. The man was alone.

After checking the license number and driver information on the patrol car's computer, the policeman returned to the van and handed the papers back. "Drive straight to your sister's now. This storm is probably going to get worse."

He headed back to his car. "That was a beautiful leather jacket laying on the passenger seat," he thought to himself. It was just like the one his wife wanted. "Maybe I should go back and ask the gentleman where he got it. No, that's a bit tacky…I'll just wait for one on sale and surprise her."

The van had disappeared when he realized he'd neglected to ask where the driver had been coming from. He did say he was going to his sister's, but what was he doing out here, on a side road no less? The officer wheeled the cruiser around.

The swirling snow made driving both difficult and dangerous on the narrow gravel side road. The wipers moved the slush and ice back and forth on the windshield, and frequently he had to roll down the window and give the wipers a snap to free them from the build up. He peered through the night down the road ahead, leaning forward over the wheel to gain a better view through the faint light of the head lamps. He almost missed it.

He had already passed the small bundle lying on the side of the road before the sight registered on his tired consciousness. That looks like a body, he suddenly thought to himself as he slammed the cruiser to a halt. He jumped from the car, grabbing his flashlight as he ran. He stooped over the snow covered mound and stared down at the bloody face of a young girl.

She was only wearing black plastic boots and a short skirt which had been pulled up around her stomach; her chest was bare. He felt for a pulse.

He felt a faint throb in her carotid artery. Without a second's hesitation he gently scooped the little form into his arms and ran back to the patrol car. He swung open the door and laid her on the seat. Taking the keys from the ignition, he quickly opened the trunk and grabbed the yellow "body blanket," still wrapped in its dust cover, from the supply case. He stripped the plastic packaging and tucked the blanket around the child.

Dropping the car into gear, he simultaneously lifted the microphone and notified the night dispatcher about what he'd discovered. Having provided what details he could, he made his way back down the narrow road and onto the highway.

Within half an hour, he pulled into the emergency ramp of the hospital. An orderly was waiting with a gurney. Nurses, doctors, and support staff instantly went into action. They rushed the girl down the corridor and into a sterile examination room. The lone officer was left to pace the hallway outside the door.

Would she make it? The first doctor who came out of the emergency room shook his head. Severe hypothermia, as well as the loss of blood, didn't give much reason for optimism.

For the next six hours she hung suspended between life and death. Her jaw, as well as her cheek bone, had been fractured. She had suffered a number of broken ribs and a punctured lung. The loss of blood from both the beating and the rape had to be replaced. Luckily the officer had rescued her before any of her fingers or toes had been frozen to the point where amputation would have been necessary. In the seventh hour, Tanya's condition stabilized.

A full day later, the little girl awakened. Sore, bruised, and still in shock, she took comfort from the white uniforms surrounding the bed and fussing over her. Within an hour after she woke up, the officer returned. Introduced by the nursing staff as the one who had found her and taken her to the hospital, she could only hold up her arms and, as he bent down to hug her, cry. She was safe.

With gentle questioning, the entire story unfolded. As soon as she revealed her name, the authorities contacted her parents, who immediately rushed to see her. There was no yelling, no accusations, no name calling— only relief, tears, and sorrow for the situation that had ended this way.

Elizabeth never returned to the street. "Tanya" died out there on that cold gravel road and Elizabeth was brought back to life.

• • •

In the two years following her ordeal, Elizabeth underwent numerous trials of her own. The arrest and conviction of the van driver provided some measure of satisfaction, but the feeling of being betrayed by Drew still remains. He is also still free. A conviction was denied.

3

Kara

The streets are a nightmare, the evilness creeps,
Hold on to your soul, 'cause you're playing for keeps.

SOMETHING was wrong. Deep inside she knew things shouldn't be this way. Her school friends were happier and more outgoing. She often wondered what caused this difference between herself and the rest of her grade nine classmates.

Activities that made other children excited only brought a questioning frown to her fourteen year old forehead. What was there to get excited about just because you had a birthday? Why did they look forward to trips with their families? How come they always ran home to show their Mom and Dad the latest test results from school? These things didn't give her a thrill or cause her to giggle with her friends.

Her eyes would fill with longing as her girlfriends' parents pulled up outside the school and placed a loving arm around a child or planted a kiss on a forehead. Kara knew she was missing out on something very special. She watched other children jump up and down with waving arms and flying hair as they described their latest triumph to a spellbound parent.

She sat alone on the school steps, shoulder leaning against the iron railing with arms crossed over her knees as she watched the last remaining child scramble into the back seat of the family car. As it pulled away, she rose to her feet, stepped onto the sidewalk, and headed down the street to her home.

Opening the back door to the duplex, Kara stepped into the kitchen. The sink full of dishes had been there since she left for school that morning. In fact, they hadn't been washed for several days. The stove was covered with pans, spoons, the dog's dish, and an assortment of plates and cups. Papers, cast off clothing, a few beer cans and dozens of cigarette butts littered the floor. Without looking she knew the refrigerator held nothing more than the remnants of takeout pizza, some sour milk, and a few wilted vegetables. The cupboard was almost bare as well.

She dropped her notebook onto the already cluttered table and walked into the front room. Her mother, dressed in old sweat pants and a T-shirt, sat on the sofa watching the last few minutes of a soap opera. Smoke from her cigarette cast a haze through the room as she glanced at the girl entering the room.

"So...have a good day?" she asked before returning her attention to the TV.

"Not too bad," replied the girl. "We finished our exams this afternoon, so no more school until September." Kara paused before continuing. "Can I stay over at Jennifer's tonight?"

"Not a chance," the woman said without looking up, "I told you to clean up this pigsty before you went to school this morning. You didn't do it, so you're grounded for the weekend!"

"But I didn't make this mess!" the girl protested. "How come I have to clean up all the time? You've been here all day—why didn't *you* clean up?"

"Because I'm sick, that's why!" the woman snapped.

"*Drunk* you mean," Kara snapped back. "I'm not cleaning up your mess!"

Her mother moved in the chair and faced her. "Your father will be home in a little while and if it isn't clean he'll teach you a lesson you won't forget!"

"He isn't my father!" the little girl countered, her voice rising. "How many times do I have to tell you that?"

"He may not be your real father, but he takes care of us, so treat him with respect!"

"I hate him! Why does he have to live here? Why can't we go back to where we used to live? Why do you always take his side and not mine?" Her little body shook with anger.

Her mother rose from the chair and faced her. Fists clenched, she advanced towards Kara. Shrinking back and covering her face with her hands, the little girl backed into the doorway.

The older woman stood looking at her daughter for several moments. She could see the fear in the way Kara cowered, could feel the anger boiling beneath the surface of her child and felt ashamed.

Her mother finally looked away, aggression draining from her body. "Because he takes care of us," she repeated softly. "Now go and clean the kitchen and get something for supper."

The girl left the room, returning to the cluttered kitchen. Banging through cupboards almost bare of food, Kara finally located a few cans of tuna fish and some macaroni. She put them in a pot and turned on the stove.

For the next half hour she busied herself cleaning the kitchen, washing the dishes and putting things back where they belonged. As she worked she had the feeling once again that things weren't right. Other kids she knew didn't have to do these jobs. Jennifer, her closest friend, had invited her to stay one night and they had just played. Jennifer's mother had cooked the supper and done the dishes. Later, the two girls talked, watched movies and shared secrets. It was the first sleep over she had been invited to and the opportunity of going again had just been denied. She leaned on the table, hands cupped under her chin as she vainly tried to figure out why her family was so different. Her preoccupation was interrupted when the rear door opened and a man entered.

"How's my little girl?" he asked striding toward her. Arms at her side, Kara went rigid as he drew her into his embrace. He gave her a quick squeeze and kissed her on the top of the head. "Got a kiss for your Dad?" he asked.

"You're not my Dad!" she replied forcefully. "You just live here!"

With a move quicker than her reactions, the man brought his fist up and hit her. The girl went through the air and landed with a thud against the corner of the table. She slowly slid to the floor. Tears filled her eyes as she struggled to rise.

"You're damned right I'm not your Dad. If I was, you'd show a little more respect! And stop that blubbering or I'll smack you again." He headed for the living room.

The little girl rose slowly to her feet and, raising her arms, wiped the tears away. Looking at her hand she saw traces of blood where her cheek had struck the edge of the table.

She finished setting the table, slowly bringing her emotions under control. It seemed she cried a lot lately. Sometimes her mother would intervene in some halfhearted fashion but tonight she never even left the sofa.

Kara slipped into her bedroom, closed the door and sat on the bed for a long time just thinking. Mentally, she tallied up the situation and, in logical fashion, listed in her mind every incident she could recall.

The man who had hit her was not her father. In fact, he was the fourth such man her mother told her to call "Father." Her mother divorced her real dad some years ago and had taken in a steady stream of losers to share her home and bed. All of them had hurt her in some way, but this latest one was the worst.

• • •

The hurting had started within days of his arrival. First the verbal assaults, words that cut deeply. He ridiculed her clothes, her voice, her freckles. Nothing escaped his scathing remarks. He called her stupid, lazy, and useless and, when he could think of nothing else to say, he would banish her to her room.

She learned to cope with the hurtful words by keeping silent. But that wouldn't satisfy the new man in her mom's life. He became physically aggressive.

It started one evening when she accidentally boiled dry a pot of potatoes. He slapped her across the face. She had cried out in surprised hurt and her mother intervened only to receive a fist in the stomach. When her mother did not immediately call the police, or throw him out, she set the pattern. Each confrontation became more abusive. Finally the ultimate indignity was forced upon Kara—the unwanted sexual advances of a man thirty years her senior.

From that moment on, her existence became one of survival. She learned quickly how to exploit others: to lie and to steal. In her own mind, she always blamed it on her stepfather.

She also learned to manipulate the man in the home. She discovered that by playing up to him she could control him. She became flirtatious, coy, and engaging. She could go from the perfect child to a demon in the time it took to brush her teeth. Teachers, counselors, and neighbors were all baffled by the seemingly split personality of this attractive child. At fourteen years old, she had learned to survive.

• • •

On this particular summer day, with a small trickle of blood oozing from the cut on her cheek, those instincts took over.

Rising from the edge of the bed, she walked to the closet and opened the bi-fold door. Reaching above the clothes, she found a small backpack she'd been saving for just such a time. Filling it with underwear, socks, some spare blouses and jeans, she took the last step in ensuring her well-being. That single step was just a small one, but it had been inevitable. She knew nothing of psychology, had never heard of Maslow's "Hierarchy of Needs," she knew only that her survival was at stake.

She opened the window and dropped the pack to the ground outside. Donning her jacket, she climbed over the ledge and dropped to the grass. There were no goodbyes, no threats of running away, no angry arguments. There were no tears of farewell, promises to stay in touch, nor any thoughts of turning back. Kara was on the run.

Keeping to the alleyways, to avoid being spotted by her mother, she ran several blocks before slowing to a walk. Even at a distance she didn't feel safe. What if he came after her? What if he dragged her back home and raped her again? The fear of going back drove away all thoughts of the future. She didn't think about the unknown dangers that would soon confront her; she only knew that what lay ahead was far less a threat than what lay behind.

A bus pass, stolen from a schoolmate, provided her with transportation to the heart of the city. She was alone, but the freedom she felt buoyed her spirits as she paced the sidewalks, still warm from the daytime sun.

As Kara moved along the streets, she spotted another girl, just slightly older than herself and also walking in an aimless manner. She caught up to her.

"Hi, watcha doin'?" she asked, as she moved into step alongside the girl.

"Just walkin'…why?" the other girl retorted, looking straight ahead.

"Just asking, that's all. I thought if you're not doing anything in particular, we could team up for a bit. Okay?"

"Sure…why not?" the other girl's response came with a shrug of her shoulders as she continued down the sidewalk.

Over the next few hours Kara, and her new friend Sandy, chatted but in the manner common to the street—they talked about neither pasts nor futures—only the present. From that restricted conversation, both learned that they were on the street for the night—neither would be returning home.

One by one, the stores locked their doors and switched on the alarms for the night. Kara and Sandy wandered aimlessly from one cafe to another.

Finally, at a dingy all-night cafeteria they drew the attention of yet another girl. This one was considerably older than the two runaways, probably in her early twenties. She waved them over to her table.

"Run way from home?" she asked bluntly. Both girls shook their heads. "Don't bullshit me, I know what's going on. You need a place to stay, right?" The directness of her question caught both girls by surprise. They looked at one another. Yes, they did need a place to stay and neither had eaten anything since noon. Both nodded in response.

"Come on with me then," she said, rising from the table. The girls followed her from the restaurant to the streets outside.

The girl, who said her name was Lisa, had a timeworn look to her face. She didn't smile or offer any lighthearted remarks or comments. She was all business. When questioned by Sandy, she only said that she lived in a nearby apartment and could put them up for a few nights.

Although a bit apprehensive with the arrangement, Kara nonetheless went along. After all, she reasoned, it certainly couldn't be as bad as it was at home!

After a ten minute walk, the three girls arrived at a small apartment block. Three story walk-ups lined the entire street and Lisa's building had nothing to distinguish it from the rest on the block. Her suite was located on the main floor facing the rear parking lot. She unlocked the door and motioned the girls inside.

Sparsely furnished, yet somewhat neat and tidy, the small place was a welcome shelter after the long evening wandering the streets. Lisa opened the cupboard and removed a glass. "Drink?" she asked, pointing first at one and then the other. Kara responded "sure" for both of them.

Lisa took a bottle of whiskey from the lower shelf and poured a generous portion into each of the three glasses on the counter. "I only have Coke," she said, more as a statement of fact than an apology, as she added the mix to the drinks.

Handing the glasses to the girls she held hers up as a toast. "To freedom."

"To freedom," Sandy and Kara replied in unison, each taking a cautious sip of the drink. The sweet drink filled Kara's mouth; she didn't anticipate the burning in her throat after she swallowed.

"So, how you gonna live?" Lisa asked.

Kara shrugged. "I don't know, I guess I'll try and get a job somewhere."

"How old are you anyway?" Lisa asked.

"Sixteen," Kara lied.

"Bullshit," came the reply. "How old are you, really?"

Kara bowed her head for a moment, wondering if she should reveal her true age. When she looked up, Lisa was waiting for her answer. "I'm fourteen," Kara finally admitted.

"And you?" Lisa asked of Sandy.

"Fifteen." she answered.

"Does anyone know where you are?" Lisa asked.

Both girls shook their heads. "Nobody cares where I am," Kara said, her voice tinged with anger. "I'm never going back home if I can help it."

"How are you going to live?" Lisa asked for the second time "You can't get a job at your age—at least not one in the regular sense."

Kara shrugged, becoming a little defensive. "I'll get by. Why do you care?"

"And you?" Lisa asked of Sandy, not bothering to give Kara a reply.

"I'll do whatever it takes," came the reply. The look of determination on Sandy's face hinted to Kara that she'd been on the streets for some time and had learned to survive. "I sell a little dope and do a few other things. People give me money if I want."

Throughout the exchange, both girls had been sipping their drinks. When Lisa poured a second round, neither objected. Kara was feeling light-headed and a little sick from not having eaten in more than twelve hours. "Any chance of getting a pizza or something?" she asked.

"Sure, just let me make a couple of calls." Lisa disappeared into the adjoining room.

The girls sat at the kitchen table continuing their conversation.

Kara learned that Sandy often got money from men. "I ain't no hooker though!" she said defensively. "I won't sell my ass for nobody. But there are ways to deal with men and get them to give you money." Kara waited for her to continue.

"You see, if you wait downtown, a lot of times men will just want company. They'll buy you a meal or give you a place to stay. All I give them though is a quick feel or at most play with them a bit—I'm not selling myself though."

Kara thought the line she drew between being a hooker and just playing with them was a fine one, but she didn't voice an opinion.

Lisa returned to the kitchen. For the first time she smiled. "I ordered some pizza and a couple of guys. We'll have a party."

This was the life, Kara thought. Booze, guys, a party. It sure beat being at home! She waited expectantly for the arrival of both the food and the boys as the girls continued to chat. Each time Kara or Sandy would bring the talk around to what Lisa did for a living, they always met with a turn in the conversation or, if they persisted, Lisa only responded with, "Oh, I get by."

Within a half-hour, a knock on the door announced the arrival of the visitors. Lisa opened the door and ushered in three young men, all in their early twenties. They set the pizza on the table, surveyed the seated pair of girls and spoke rapidly to each other in a foreign language.

Lisa introduced Kara and Sandy. The men gave their names as Peter, Tran, and what sounded like Huay. Lisa immediately took Peter by the arm and proudly announced that they were members of The Young Circle Boys. "The infamous gang," she laughed. She rolled up Peter's sleeve and displayed a tattoo of a fire-breathing winged dragon on the upper portion of his biceps.

"Turn around," she told Peter and, when he did, she lifted up his shirt showing large and intricate tattoos covering his back. "He says these give him power," she announced.

She then exhibited the tattoos on Tran and Huay for the girls. Kara was both repulsed and fascinated. She'd heard about "Asian gangs" on the news, but never met any. She felt a twinge of fear.

The men had brought cocaine but, when it was offered, Kara refused. Sandy immediately put the straw to her nose and "did a line," as did Lisa. Kara lit a cigarette instead and continued sipping her whiskey. The pizza felt heavy in her stomach, but at least she wasn't hungry.

Lisa invited everyone into the living room where they settled into various chairs and sofas. Peter drew Lisa down onto his lap and they started kissing and fondling. Tran sat beside Sandy and Huay pulled Kara down beside him. In a few minutes Peter and Lisa disappeared into the adjoining bedroom, leaving the other four behind.

It didn't take much to figure out what was going to happen. The two men immediately started trying to kiss and touch the two girls. Sandy offered only token resistance, then responded to Tran's advances. Kara kept pushing her "date" away, insisting that she was not interested.

When Huay pulled back on his advances and settled back onto the couch, Kara relaxed. Under his skillful questioning, she told him her past—something she'd never done before with anyone. He learned that she had few friends, a violent relationship with her family, and no relatives she felt she could call upon. He asked to see a picture of her mother and she dug through her knapsack. The photo was tucked inside a little phone book where she kept the numbers of her social worker, her aunt and uncle, and several others. Listed among the numbers were the names of the few friends she had made in school, a guy she met at the roller rink, as well as others she couldn't recall.

Midnight passed and she grew to enjoy the company. They shared stories and she learned that Huay, Peter, and Tran were constantly on the move: from Los Angeles to New York, from Toronto to Vancouver, and from Houston to Saigon, they literally traveled the world. They had little fear of, and no respect for, the legal system or any other form of control. Kara was intrigued. To be able to travel, to be free, to do the things she wanted to do with no interference. That was living!

By breakfast time, the three men were on the move—this time with Kara and Sandy. They hadn't asked if the girls wanted to go, but rather took them by the arms and led them to a car. Isolated and frightened, the girls' objections were ignored as the men piled their meager belongings unceremoniously in the back seat. Weakly, both girls voiced their hesitation, but the sheer size and power of their escorts overcame their will to resist.

Seizing Kara by the shoulders, Huay looked deep into her eyes and told her in words that could not be misunderstood, that they were going to another city. He grabbed her travel pack and dug through it until he found her address book. Telling her he would "Hang onto it so she didn't lose it," he cut off all hope of contacting someone she knew. She knew that with her little book, he possessed the phone numbers and addresses of anyone who would help her—or anyone who cared.

As they traveled west she grew increasingly afraid. Try as she might, she could get no information about what was in store. She was helpless.

They continued their trip, stopping only for gas and snacks. There was no question in Kara's mind that she was a prisoner. What they intended to do, or where they were taking her and Sandy, she had no idea. She began to plan.

As she dozed off and on in the rear seat, she laid out her thoughts. They drew further into the night and she could sense the three men becoming more confident. Little slips in their concentration began to appear. At the start of the trip, first one of them would accompany Sandy or Kara everywhere, even to the bathroom, but, as the hours passed, they just kept an eye on her from the car, allowing the girls more freedom. She waited. The journey settled down into a routine of monotonous driving, interspersed by brief stops for fuel and personal needs.

Just after midnight, as they traveled through yet another nameless town, Kara spotted a police cruiser pull out onto the pavement behind them. It sped up and kept pace for several miles. Huay, driving for the third time, did not look in the mirror as he drove down the deserted road. After about five minutes of following them, the driver of the police car turned on the red and blue flashing lights and moved up closer behind them. This was her chance!

Huay slowed the powerful Ford slightly. Kara reached for the door handle. She would jump when the car slowed, she decided, and run off into the bush beside the road. The men in the car wouldn't follow her with the police right behind, and she could wait for them to leave and come out of the bush and get help from the police. She gathered her coat tighter around herself and prepared for the car to slow down sufficiently. Instead, she felt a hard object pushed brutally into her side. She looked down and saw the barrel of a revolver in Peter's hand. He said something to Huay and the car accelerated.

The patrol car was no match for the power under the hood of the Ford. They pulled ahead rapidly and the lights of their pursuer fell behind. The men were ecstatic. Huay banged his hands on the wheel and laughed. Peter slapped his back and returned the gun to his pocket. Tran grinned from his seat in the front and said something the girls could not understand.

After a few miles, Huay turned off the highway and continued on a secondary road. For the rest of the trip, they moved from one road to another, successfully avoiding the police. When the sun rose in the east, they arrived at their destination—a run down motel in the inner city. Tran left the car, spoke to the manager, and returned a few moments later with a key.

They parked the car in front of the room and they hoisted their bags inside. Peter ordered some food from a nearby takeout restaurant and, after the food arrived, he made several more calls. By the time they'd eaten, a number of men arrived.

Greeting each other, the men's conversation was animated, friendly, and familiar. It was obvious that they traveled in the same circle of acquaintances. They motioned the two girls to stand and the men looked them over.

One reached forward and grasped Sandy's arm. She slapped his hand away and he immediately kicked her in the stomach. He spoke angrily to her, while the other men laughed. Roughly he threw her down on the bed and tore her clothes off. Rolling her onto her stomach and holding her tightly around the waist, he viciously raped her from behind. Her screams died to pitiful moans, as the man finished and zippered up his pants. There was no question now about who held the power.

Sandy didn't struggle as she was led outside to a waiting car. The party continued and one of the men produced several bottles of alcohol and a second unwrapped several folded decks of cocaine. Another man had shoved Kara onto the bed while the man had raped Sandy, but no one else had touched her.

After Sandy had been taken from the motel, Kara withdrew into herself, sitting immobile on the bed while the men around her spoke in their own language. They were in no hurry. She wasn't going anywhere and the combination of drugs and alcohol they had each taken seemed more important to them than the huddled child on the soiled bed. Maybe they'll forget about me she thought to herself. Maybe they just wanted Sandy. They hadn't revealed their intentions, but the way they had treated Sandy had all but extinguished her hopes.

As all people do in moments of uncontrollable fear, she grasped for any sign—however minute—that they would leave her alone. Each time one looked out the window, each time there was another bottle opened or a new line of coke snorted, she prayed that it would be the action that would precede their departure. She raised her eyes, peeking through the strands of hair that had fallen over her face. The four of them were now occupying their time playing a kind of game with ivory tiles. Each tile had a marking on it and the game was fast and loud. She moved to the foot of the bed, determined to escape.

With a bound she dove to the door and grasped the handle. It was locked. As she struggled to turn the lock and then opened the door, she heard laughing behind her. She turned, fully expecting that one or more of them would be upon her, dragging her back into the room. She was surprised when no one seemed to notice her leaving and no one tried to block her escape. She bolted to the street, then stopped.

She stood on the sidewalk outside and her fears began to diminish. Why had they just let her go? Maybe she had mistaken their intentions after all. Maybe they were just there to party. She wondered if she should go back and wait for Sandy. She shook her head. She had been so scared since the day before when they left Lisa's apartment—she only wanted to get as far away as possible.

Kara walked for miles. Her feet were sore, her head ached, and she still felt unsettled by the experience in the motel. She moved into the center of the city, satisfied that she had once again gained her freedom, but not knowing how she was going to survive in this strange environment. She spotted a sign for the subway and walked down the steps to the landing platform. It was almost deserted. Only a few late night stragglers leaned against the walls waiting for the next train. She moved to the edge of the platform and looked down the tracks. The single headlight of the oncoming train glowed far down the dark reaches of the tunnel.

She turned to move back from the edge and bumped into a figure standing close behind her. About to apologize and move out of the way, she looked up into the cold dark eyes of a man. Before she could move away from him, he grasped her roughly by the arm.

A second man stepped to her far side and took her other arm. They walked to the edge of the platform without speaking and held the little girl out over the tracks of the oncoming train. As it rushed forward she felt the grip on one of her arms loosen and she started to fall. Twisting she grasped the sleeve of the one remaining man and pulled herself back to safety. He grinned as she scrambled to regain her balance. He kept hold of her one arm and walked back down the platform, dragging Kara with him up the stairs and onto the street. His partner walked several paces behind.

Why had the men let her leave the motel? How did they know where she was? Why were these men sent to get her? Her head spun with questions as they placed her in the back seat of a small import car. The taller one, the man who had let her slip on the platform, drove the car and the other sat in the back seat beside her. She could only conclude that someone had followed her and knew every step she made, every corner she took and every person she saw. There was no place to hide and no place to run. She couldn't even make a phone call; she had never retrieved the little phone book that Huay took from her.

They drove deep into old Chinatown. She didn't know if her two captors spoke English or not, but they certainly did not speak to her. They muttered briefly to one another in their native tongue, but it was obvious it was only to share directions and questions, not to engage in any long dialogue. The car turned into an alley and came to a stop at the rear of a ramshackle building. A wooden staircase wound its way from the clutter to a lighted doorway on the second floor.

The three left the car, the tall one leading the way. They climbed to the door and entered. The hallway was long, ending in a common area with a number of smaller rooms running off the perimeter. Kara was taken to one of the compartments and waved inside.

The room had a single bed, a straight backed chair, a wash stand, and a small closet. She sat on the bed, confused and disoriented. She had no clothes other than the ones she was wearing. She had no money, no purse, no make up nor any personal belongings. She was utterly, desperately alone.

She may have sat on the bed for minutes or hours. The passage of time was meaningless. The door opened and a woman in her late forties entered the room. Kara felt elated. At last here was someone who could explain what was happening—maybe someone to help. She stood and was about to speak when the woman pushed her back onto the bed.

"Strip," was all the woman said.

The last remaining scrap of free will drained from her body as she removed her clothes and returned to a sitting position on the bed. Modesty was something that she no longer cared about and the woman's critical gaze did not cause Kara the discomfort or embarrassment it might have only a few weeks earlier.

With a grunt and the woman uttered, "Don't move," and left the room. Kara remained seated. She soon returned and delivered a tray with juice, a hamburger, and an orange. She ate the food, more from habit than from hunger, long passed the point where food held any importance.

When she finished, she placed the tray on the floor. Taking a blanket from the bed, she wrapped it around herself like a cape. She moved to the door and tried the knob. It was locked. She lay down exhausted, and pulling the covers over her head, fell into a troubled sleep.

Startled awake as the door swung open, Kara saw an older man enter the room. He grasped the edge of the blanket covering her and pulled it down. Terrified, the little girl could only lie there, her body exposed to his cold stare. She moved to get out of the bed and he once again pushed her down. He stood in front of her and removed his clothes, piling them on the one chair in the corner of the tiny room. Then he held her down and lay on top of her.

He was the first of thirteen men that night. After the first few, she blanked the violations of her body from her mind. She was not a novice to sex, having been used as a pliable object since she had been first raped by her stepfather, but she had never experienced anything like this. If the men thought she was not active enough, they bit her frail shoulders or pinched the inside of her thighs. If she cried out or jumped, they enjoyed it all the more. She quickly learned to respond with her voice and her body.

Sunlight streamed through the single window as the last man left the room. She was bleeding from the shoulder where the bites had penetrated the skin. Her thighs were black and blue and the red blister on her right breast gave mute evidence to the man—she couldn't remember which— who had held a lighted cigarette to her body as she lay beneath him.

She had no idea of the passage of time. It could have been a few hours or a few days since they took her to the room; she didn't know or care. This was not something she had expected when she ran away from home. The horrors she had undergone in the time since she had made that fateful decision had blurred her memory. The only thought she could hold onto was the idea of escaping. She had tried twice, once when the police were following the car and the second time from the motel; neither attempt had been successful. They seemed to know every move she made, every thought that went through her mind. She wanted to die.

She tried the door; it remained locked. She looked through the window into the alley below. Although it was two floors down, she thought she could jump without too much difficulty. She put her two small hands under the window casing and lifted. It was stuck! She struggled for several more moments before she realized that nails were embedded into the window frame, preventing it from being opened. She cried with frustration. Was there no escape? She returned to the bed and sat on the edge, her thin body shivering in the chilly room. She pulled the blanket around herself, shoulders hunched. She grasped the edge of the wrap and pulled it tightly across her chest. She stared out the window.

Kara stood and paced around the room. She began looking under the bed, pulling the covers back and examining the mattress. She moved to the wash stand and pulled at the taps. They were tight. Finally she moved to the chair and, picking it up, walked purposefully to the window. Hefting the chair, she smashed the glass, letting a burst of fresh air into the room. She was about to pick the shards of glass from the frame and climb through the small opening when she looked down into the alley one more time. There were three men down below looking up at her, laughing. She was trapped!

Tears streamed down her cheeks as she backed away. She was alone— without help, without hope. In the midst of the shattered glass she sank to the floor and wept, sobbing deep agonizing cries as finally, irrevocably, she understood the finality of her situation. She would never again know sunshine. Never see her mother, her friends or her teachers. She would never have the chance to play, to be just a little girl.

She looked at the floor where she lay curled into a tight little ball. A six inch shard of glass lay within her grasp. Running the razor sharp edge over her wrist the sight of blood coming from the thin cut fascinated her. She watched the steady drip of scarlet falling to the floor and began to feel a sense of peace. Welcome sleep settled over her and Kara slowly stretched out on the floor. She was finally free.

4

Jackie

You think we want freedom? You think we want drugs, booze and parties?
You think we want to be here?
Let me tell you what we want. We just want to be kids.

THE babble of voices and the racking of cue balls provided a backdrop as Jackie lined up a crucial shot. She leaned against the table, cue stick held lightly in her hands, eyes sighting down the length of the stick. A man disengaged from the group at the bar and moved across the floor.

"Hi, little one," he said, sliding up behind her.

Jackie looked over her shoulder as she felt his body press up against hers. She smiled as she recognized the man as the same one who had held the door to the pool room open for her earlier in the evening. "Hi, yourself," she replied, turning back to the table and her next shot.

As she lined up to complete a combination to the corner pocket, she felt the man put his arms around her and move his hands down the stick, guiding her on the shot. He steadied her aim, and she snapped the shot away, sending the eight ball to the target with enough spin to bring the cue ball back from the black and away from the danger of a scratch.

"Yes!" she yelled, turning and giving her assistant a glowing smile. "Thanks for the help." She collected the small wager sitting on the rail, and moved back to where she had left her drink and cigarettes. He followed her and sat down across the table from her.

She lit a cigarette, leaned back in her chair and eyed her companion. Older, probably in his mid-twenties she thought. His long hair tied in a pony tail, the man wore a black cut off T-shirt and oil-stained jeans covering low-rider boots. The watch strap on his left wrist was festooned with silver studs, each adornment reflecting the light from the bright overhead lamps. He wore large silver rings of odd shapes and designs. One was in the form of a skull, another was inscribed with the logo of a well-known motorcycle manufacturer. Several others were of ambiguous design.

The man noticed her looking at his rings. He held up his hands to allow a better view. She took his hands in hers, turning them over for a better view. "They would sure hurt if you hit someone wouldn't they?" she observed. He laughed, "I guess they would, but I'd never hit a pretty girl like you. I've seen you here for the last few nights...what's your name?"

"Jackie," came the reply. "I've seen you, too. Do you always hang around here?"

"Not usually. I came in to see a guy about something and noticed you all by yourself, so I came back. You with someone?"

"No, I just enjoy hanging out here. The bar staff let me in—even though I'm not eighteen. I don't get hassled, so I keep coming back."

"Want some weed?" he asked, placing his elbows on the table.

The abrupt change in the conversation caught her by surprise. "Sure. Why not?" After all, she thought, I'm here for a good time, might as well try a few things out.

He stood and signaled her to accompany him.

When they reached the warmth of late evening outside they passed through a gathering of young girls and guys sitting on the steps, leaning against the wall or wandering around the parking lot. As usual there were a number of cars occupied by couples or small groups. The two walked to the far corner of the lot.

Expecting a flashy car of some sort, Jackie was surprised when the man inserted his key in the lock of a beat up older model. In spite of her surprise, she willingly slipped into the front seat, as he courteously held open the door for her.

He moved around the hood of the car and slid in behind the wheel. Settling back in the seat, he turned on the radio. Dialing a soft rock station, he reached up under the dash and retrieved one of the tightly rolled marijuana cigarettes stashed there. It was twisted at both ends and stained along the side where he had licked it.

Surprisingly, this was Jackie's first exposure to any form of drug. Raised in a religious home, she had escaped exposure to the drug culture, due mostly to what she described as her "goody-goody" family. "Have you ever tried it?" the man asked. Jackie shook her head.

"You gotta puff it quickly or it goes out." He placed it between his lips and, flicking a lighter, coaxed the joint to life. He toked deeply, holding the smoke in his lungs to maximize the effect. Grasping the smoldering cigarette between his thumb and forefinger, he offered it to her. She took the offered joint and puffed quickly. "No," he laughed. "If you puff it like that, it'll just burn up. You gotta inhale!"

She mimicked his earlier actions, dragging deeply on the joint, taking the acrid smoke deep in her lungs. It had a strange, almost sweet taste.

"So, what's your name?" Jackie asked as she passed the joint back to him.

"Roach."

Jackie giggled. The effects of the marijuana were starting to tell. "No, I mean your name, not what we're smoking!"

He smiled. "That *is* my name—at least that's what everyone calls me. It's been so long since I used my real name, can't even remember it myself sometimes."

He took another drag and passed it back. "So, what are you doing down here?"

"Just having fun. My folks are away on holidays so I came down to the hall with my girlfriend to shoot some pool a couple of days ago. You must have seen her...long black hair, kinda skinny?" He nodded in response.

She offered back the smoke and he waved it off. "You go ahead, it'll make you feel happy."

He rolled down the window to allow the smoke to leave the car. "Wanna go for a ride?"

"Sure," Jackie replied, leaning back into the seat and letting the pleasant sensations wash over her.

Roach started the engine and left the parking lot. Heading downtown he kept the conversation going with a steady stream of questions about her past, what she was doing now, her school, her friends, and her interests.

He learned that she was a good student, enjoyed school, was popular, and didn't seem to have too many problems at home—at least none that were significantly different from any other young teenager. He did learn that her parents were fundamentalists and kept a tight rein on their only daughter.

The evening passed and they shared another joint from the supply hidden beneath the dash. Jackie felt comfortable in the company of the older man. He treated her with respect, listened to her as she related her life's story, and sympathized as she expressed her frustrations over the tight restrictions placed on her by her parents. The time flew by quickly, and their conversation, while somewhat one-sided, was nonetheless enjoyable.

Midnight came and went. They stopped at a hamburger stand, and he bought her some fries and a double cheeseburger, along with a coke. She was hungry now. "Got the munchies" as he put it, and she quickly devoured the meal. As they left the restaurant and drove towards her home he asked for her phone number. Dropping her off in front of her home, he secured the promise that she would be down at the pool hall the following night.

Each evening for the next week, Jackie was a regular at the pool hall. Nightly she would meet with Roach, share a few of his joints, and they would drive around or go have something to eat. She felt very grown up sitting beside him and was impressed by the respect other patrons of the hall showed him.

He generously shared his supply of marijuana with her and towards the end of the week gave her a dime bag containing a quantity of marijuana, "In case I miss you some evening."

During that thrill-filled summer he took Jackie to a steady parade of parties. There was always plenty of booze and marijuana and, without hesitation, she accepted the addition of a number of pills to her increasing appetite for drugs. She never paid for them, so she didn't worry about her parents finding out about her drug use through an increase in her spending habits.

Almost every evening, and certainly every weekend, she would seek out Roach, and after spending an hour or so with him, would be blasted. She took increasing amounts of narcotics, mixing the various pills with booze people gave her at the parties.

Her parents returned from their vacation and noticed the change in their daughter. When the initial inquiries of concern met with open hostility, they let the matter drop feeling that it was "'just a phase she was going through" and that maybe when she got back into school in September, things would return to normal.

The fall semester began and, temporarily, things did seem to change. Activities related to school took up some of Jackie's time and reconnecting with old friends seemed to settle her down somewhat. But the excitement she had enjoyed during the summer months was lacking and she found she could only cope effectively if she had a regular supply of drugs. She spoke to Roach on the telephone daily.

When she felt the pressing need to have a "hit," she would meet him at a nearby convenience store and he would give her a bag of weed, some uppers or a few prescription drugs that he had managed to score through his contacts. These were usually enough to get her through the week and, as the leaves on the maple trees turned from green to orange and gold, she met him with increasing frequency.

On the 26th of November, she arrived home from school to find that her parents had prepared a surprise fourteenth birthday party for her. The front room was decorated with streamers and balloons and her mother had invited a number of friends over to celebrate the occasion. Jackie was delighted. She reveled in the attention she received from her friends and family and was ecstatic with her various gifts, especially a gold locket on a chain from her parents.

After the last guest left, Jackie went to her room. Digging through her underwear drawer, she located the small vial of capsules that Roach had given to her earlier in the week. It was empty. Panic started to rise inside her. She needed something. After all, wasn't this her birthday? Didn't she have a right to get stoned? She picked up the phone and dialed Roach's number.

"Hi, can I come over to see you?" she asked.

"Well," came the reply, "It's late. Can you put it off until the morning?"

"No, I need some stuff now—not tomorrow!" The whining in her voice revealing to an experienced listener just how dependent she had become on the mind-altering substances.

After agreeing to meet Roach at a downtown cafe, Jackie hung up the phone. She was excited. She would be able to celebrate her birthday in grand style. Roach would take care of everything!

They met at the restaurant. Jackie arrived alone. As she walked to a table near the rear, she saw that this time—unlike every other occasion they met—another man accompanied Roach. Although dressed similarly to Roach, this guy was larger, with a full beard and a large stomach. He was wearing the colors of a local motorcycle club.

Jackie took a seat beside Roach, directly across the table from the large biker. She turned to Roach and whispered, "Did you bring some stuff for me? I really need it! Today's my birthday!" Roach put his hand over Jackie's mouth. "Not so loud. Do you want everyone to hear what we're talking about? Before I give you any more, I think you should know something."

Roach pointed across the table at the other man. "Jackie, meet Doug. He's the guy who's been giving me all the weed and shit that you've been doing the last few months." Doug nodded in response to the introduction, staring silently into Jackie's face. "He's been keeping tally on how much you've been given. Any idea how much money you owe him?"

Jackie's mouth went dry. She shook her head.

"About six thousand dollars worth. Can you believe that?"

"Six thousand dollars? I don't have that kind of money! I thought you were just giving it to me. You never said anything about having to buy it. How come you want it now?"

Doug spoke for the first time. "We don't want it all right now, just a little so we know that you are not trying to weasel out on us. How about a thousand by next week? Is that okay?"

Jackie was stunned. "A thousand dollars? Where am I going to get a thousand dollars?" She looked from Roach to Doug.

"Look, little lady. I couldn't give a shit where you come up with the money. You've been freeloading off the good nature of my friend Roach here all summer. He's too softhearted. You wanted the stuff...and he gave it to you. But everything has a price. What did you think? That you were getting it for free and never had to pay for it?"

Jackie could only nod. She felt like such a jerk. Of course she had known that drugs cost money. It just never crossed her mind that she would have to pay for them. She thought that Roach was just being nice.

"Okay—I'll try to get the money by next week. But what happens if I can't get the money? Can I have more time to pay?"

Doug rose, his massive knuckles pressed against the table top. His immense frame seemed to fill the corner of the small cafe. He reached down and lifted Jackie's chin, his eyes boring into hers.

"Don't even *think* about not paying. You know who we are by now, and if you think we're just going to forget about a little debt, you have another thought coming! You have the thousand here by next week or you'll wish you'd never met us."

Jackie could only sit there and tremble. Looking into his eyes, she knew that somehow, some way, she would have to come up with the money. There was no doubt in her mind that Doug would carry through with his threats. Over the summer, she had attended a number of parties with Roach and learned that he was "a striker," a rookie member of a local motorcycle gang. He had to do the bidding of the more senior members—like Doug.

With a last menacing look at Jackie, Doug pushed away from the table and left the cafe. "I can't get a thousand dollars by next week Roach. What am I going to do?" Jackie's voice trembled.

"Not to worry, we'll think of something. Here." He handed her a yellow-jacket capsule. "On the house, so to speak." Jackie took the offering gratefully.

The week passed in a blur. Jackie couldn't concentrate on her work at school and the slightest comment from her parents would send her into a fit of hysterical crying. She would not respond to their concerns, at every turn shutting them out of her thoughts. Throughout the week, she only slept fitfully and did not eat. By Saturday she was a mess.

Once again, she returned to Roach. In her hand, she clutched the hundred dollars that she had stolen from her father's wallet. She gave it to her contact. He accepted the money and simply asked, "Where's the rest?"

She shook her head in desperation. "That's all I could get. Is there any way I can have some more time to pay?"

Roach glared at her. "You've had ample time to pay. Doug gave you a big break not asking for it all at once. Remember—you owe him six grand. All you've given on account is a piddling one hundred dollars. He ain't gonna be happy, I can tell you that."

"Is there anything I can do? Any way I can get out of this? I mean, you never told me I had to pay, otherwise I wouldn't have run up that kind of debt!"

"There might be one way we can work this out," Roach speculated, looking away from her.

"How? I'll do anything!...Anything!"

Jackie didn't understand that those words were to change her life forever. She did not realize at that moment that every pill she had taken from Roach, every cube of hash, every lump of chocolate mescaline, every Thai stick, had been an investment by him. And now the dividends of that investment were about to be cashed in.

"Well, there is something...I don't know if you can do it...I'll have to ask Doug and see if he'd be willing. You'll have to work real hard and do as you're told if you expect us to forget about that six thousand!"

"Please ask him...okay?" Jackie looked at Roach expectantly.

Roach left the table and walked to the pay phone on the wall. He dialed a number from memory and, as Jackie watched, appeared to be arguing with the person on the other end of the line. He looked at her often, gesturing with his hands and when he hung up the receiver gave her the thumbs-up signal that everything had been worked out.

"All right. Doug wasn't too pleased, but I think I talked him into it."

"What do I have to do?"

"I'll tell you in the car on the way over." Saying that, Roach dropped several dollars on the scarred table to pay for the coffee and, with Jackie in tow, headed for the parking lot. The drive wasn't long, just sufficient for Jackie to begin to worry that she had involved herself in something that was rapidly getting beyond her control. She relaxed a little when she questioned Roach further and he replied that it was "just a party" they were going to.

They pulled up to a run down motel, just off the downtown core. It had once been a picturesque little place—the kind one sees in most tourist towns—with a small office out front and a parking lot encircled on three sides by a one story row of suites. Roach drove past the office and parked in front of one of the units.

He faced Jackie. "This is where you earn your keep. I'll let you inside and in a few minutes a man will arrive. I want you to treat him real good. If you do, the first thousand you owe us will be marked paid on account. It's only one man...and you'll have to do him. I don't want any complaining, no bitching, no nuthin'. Understand?"

Jackie understood all right. He expected her to have sex with a total stranger! She turned to Roach, her voice both fearful and pleading. "I can't do that. I can't go in there and have sex with some guy I don't even know! What if he gives me a disease or something?" She slumped down in the seat.

Roach lunged over and grabbed her by the hair. She yelped as he pulled her across the seat until her face was just inches from his own. She shook with fear as he explained in clipped words just what it was she was going to do—not expected to do—*going* to do!

"Listen you little bitch. I've just about had it with you. You owe us six thousand dollars. Now if you want to get your pretty ass kicked by Doug and some of the other guys, just keep screwing me around. I went out on a limb for you tonight because you couldn't come up with the thousand bucks." He sneered, mimicking her voice of earlier. "'I'll do anything. *Anything.*' Isn't that what you said? Well baby, time's up. If you jack me around now, I'll not only turn you over to Doug and his group, I will personally go to your Mom and Dad. They might like to know just what you were up to this summer while they were laying back enjoying the sunshine, thinking their pure little girl was staying home and chatting on the phone. I'll tell them about the parties where you didn't think it was so horrible if you had sex with someone. And what about the drugs? What do you think they'll say about that, huh? And then, after I tell them all that, the six thousand will still have to be paid. Maybe I'll take it out on your old lady? Maybe she'd like a little roll in the hay with me?"

Roach continued for several minutes, describing in exacting detail what he would do to Jackie's mother. By the time he had finished, she was sobbing. Her chest heaving with racking breaths, she tried to talk.

"Wha...wha...what will I have to do besides have sex with the one man?" she asked.

"You'll do whatever I say. Tonight, just the one guy, but there's no way any piece of tail is worth six grand. In fact, just because I had to put myself out to get you outta this jam, I'm going to add another $500 charge to your debt. That's for all my troubles in setting this up." Without waiting for a reply, he opened the door and walked around to her side of the car. He jerked open the door and dragged her out.

Walking up to the room, he stopped just before entering. "You better look like you're enjoying this. You have to smile and make the guy feel special. If you don't, I'll know about it and you'll wish you'd have done like I told you. Do ya understand what I'm saying? I'm not screwing around with you any more bitch, you'll do as you're told and do it right. Ya understand?"

Jackie was stunned by what had taken place over the last half hour. Her mind had not absorbed all the changes taking place and Roach's transformation from a fun-time friend to a vicious, demanding pimp. She could only nod. He opened the door to the run down motel room and pushed her inside in front of him.

There was no one there. She felt a momentary relief that the stranger had not arrived yet. Maybe he wouldn't show up at all!

Roach entered the room behind her. He quickly checked the room including the small bath area and returned to Jackie. "He'll be here in about ten minutes. I'm going to be just outside in the car to make sure he doesn't get too rough with you." He put his arms around her and pulled her to his chest.

Cradling her face in his hands he forced her to look up. He again spoke gently to her. "Look, little one, I know you feel bad about this, but so do I! Just be good to the trick and you'll be down a thousand bucks in just a few minutes. A couple more evenings and you'll be debt free!"

Jackie was young, but not naive, and she knew that she was being manipulated by an expert. His facade of gentleness was just that, a facade used to secure her compliance. In spite of this new awareness, she wrapped her arms around him, pressing the side of her face to his chest. She nodded. "Okay, Roach I'll do it."

"Atta girl." He moved her back to arms length. "And one more thing. Don't even think of leaving. I'll be outside and if I see you leave, I'll drag you back and I'll make you so sorry, you'll beg to work for me." Saying that, he walked to the door and left the room.

Jackie laid her light jacket over the back of the single chair located near the battered desk. She placed her purse under the bed; there was no way she was going to get ripped off on top of being raped! It was clear in her mind that this was rape—she didn't want to do it but was being forced to have sex against her will. She went into the bathroom to wipe her eyes and put on some makeup.

The door opened as she left the bathroom. The man was in his early fifties, gray hair curling above his collar. It was obvious from his clothes, manicure, and confidence that he enjoyed success in his business, whatever that is, Jackie thought.

The preliminaries took but a moment and then the act itself. As the john completed his part of the coupling, Jackie pushed him off from on top of her and ran into the bathroom. She slammed the door and leaned against the coolness of the wood. Naked, she stood and cried, slowly lowering herself to the floor where she sat, back leaning against the door, elbows on her raised knees, and the palms of her hands pressed against her face. She felt so dirty! Never in her life had she felt so filthy, so degraded. She also knew that, as much as she might wish it, this was only the start. The original six thousand dollars that she owed Roach and Doug might now be reduced by a thousand, but the addition of the five hundred dollar "street fee" had, in reality, only slightly reduced the total.

She heard the door to the room close. She quickly washed herself and opened the bathroom door. The man had gone, but she could hear voices outside. It sounded as if the man was talking to Roach. A car door slammed and a car left the lot.

The door opened once again. This time, however, Doug entered the room. He stood just inside the door, slowly reached behind him and closed the door, never taking his eyes off her. Jackie rapidly struggled into her clothes. Doug spoke softly and menacingly. "Leave them off."

She ignored him and continued buttoning her blouse. In a stride he was in front of her.

"I said leave them off!" His voice rising, "Now leave them off!" He shoved her onto the bed. She started to rise.

She never saw the blow coming. With a closed fist he hit her just below the rib cage, knocking the wind from her lungs and leaving her gasping for breath. She doubled over on the bed; her only thought was to get one more breath. She felt herself strangling; each small gulp of air burned as she forced it down into her aching lungs.

Doug stood above her screaming in anger. "Don't you ever defy me, bitch. Don't even think of it! You know what you are? A bitch with an *attitude*! That's what you are and we're going to change that right now."

He walked over to the coat rack and ripped a wire coat hanger from the rod. He twisted the hook until the tightly wrapped wire unraveled. He straightened out the hanger then doubled it over in the middle. Holding the two ends in his large hand, the doubled portion protruded from his grasp.

Still struggling to regain her breath, Jackie started to tremble violently when she saw the hanger. She recognized the wire as a "pimp stick." At one of the parties she'd been to during the summer, she had heard someone joking about it and how a pimp had used it on one of his girls. This time, however, she didn't laugh. This time she knew it was for her.

She screamed and scrambled across the bed towards the door. As she sprawled across the bed to reach the other side, she heard the whistle of the wire, followed immediately by an indescribable pain on the back of her thighs. She screamed again and again as the thin metal bit into the backs of her thighs, her buttocks and her lower back.

"Shut up, slut, and take it!" Doug yelled. "The more you yell, the harder it'll be on you." He grabbed her and pulled her back onto the bed. He rolled her over onto her back. He held her down, pushing his hand against her chest.

"Shut up now, or I'll do more than just give you a whippin'."

Jackie clamped her mouth shut, stifling the cries of pain. She could only stare, terrified, into the face of Doug hovering only inches above her own.

She nodded.

He released her and stood back. "I talked to the trick that was just in here. He didn't think you were worth what he paid for you." His voice dripped with scorn. "He didn't like your attitude. He thought you were a little pig in fact: no style, no movement. No nuthin'. Next time, and believe me there will be a next time, you better show some life. These guys pay good money for you and you better not disappoint them. You do and you'll get a whipping or worse each time until we get you trained. Understand?"

Jackie nodded. She did understand. She understood that she had somehow landed in the middle of something that was far worse than she could have imagined even in her worst dreams. These guys played for keeps. Any hopes she had before about paying off the money and getting out seemed to be fading quickly. As if reading her mind, Doug continued.

"Just for this little dust up, I'm going to wipe the credit you earned tonight completely away. You might have lost me a good customer. You still owe the six grand, plus the five hundred dollars to Roach for his troubles. Now, get your clothes on."

Painfully, Jackie stood and put on her clothes. The welts on her back, buttocks and thighs, while incredibly painful, were not bleeding, but the agony of tugging her slacks over the blistered flesh brought more tears to her eyes. She clamped her teeth over her lips to keep from crying out.

They left the run down motel, Jackie moving as quickly as her sore body would allow. Roach was seated in the driver's seat of the car, engine running, as they crossed the cement. Doug opened the front passenger door and shoved Jackie onto the seat. He leaned in and spoke to Roach.

"Keep the bitch in line. Take her over to the house and have Cindy keep an eye on her for the rest of the night." As Jackie pulled her feet into the car, he slammed the door.

The drive over to Cindy's house was silent. Any remaining thoughts of escape that Jackie might have had were wiped away as Roach leaned over and locked the door. Within a half-hour they pulled into a driveway.

"Okay...here's where you'll be staying for a while. This is Cindy's place. She's Doug's main and she'll take care of your back. Don't screw around with her, or Doug will find out and tune you up again. The next time he might not be so easy on you."

Jackie remained with Cindy for the next three days. During this short stay, it became clearer what her role would be in the immediate future. A number of the members of the motorcycle club came to the house, discussing "business." These discussions, always conducted quietly and away from the women, were far reaching and on varied topics. Unknown to Jackie, there were a number of young girls stashed away at various locations throughout the city.

In previous years, bikers had used mature women to work the prostitution strolls in most major cities. With the johns' changing taste for younger flesh, however, the bikers, ever aware of business opportunities, responded to the market and were now adapting to those shifts in merchandising sex. The high visibility of traditional street prostitutes was now becoming a political issue as law enforcement, social welfare agencies, and the community in general, took decisive steps to reduce both the number of prostitutes and the profit motive of those predators who reaped the benefits of their cash transactions.

Cities implemented numerous rescue programs, and established schools and nurseries. These actions, coupled with a victimology approach by law enforcement, all contributed to a large number of women leaving the life of prostitution and "signing" on those who had exploited them. The pimps were increasingly nervous about their control over women who were working the streets and changes were called for. Thus the shift to juvenile girls—and stashing them off the street. The younger ones were easier to control, they satisfied the increasing market demand and, with a rise in the population euphemistically called "street kids," times were ripe for these changes.

Jackie was only one of a growing number of young women forced into servitude. But this didn't matter to Jackie. She was not privy to those clandestine meetings, and even if she had been included, it would have mattered not a wit; she was now one of the new girls in Doug's "stable." Roach, who'd brought her into the life and "bumped" her for Doug, was off to new targets. She would not see much of her old boyfriend in the weeks ahead and when she did, he was not the supportive, kindly man who had showed her a good time and supplied all of the drugs the past exciting summer.

During the late fall, her pimp moved Jackie from house to house as her involvement in the life of an "inside prostitute" became entrenched. He would place her with Cindy and Doug for several days, then with some of the other girls working for him. She dressed in the clothes she was given to wear, dyed her hair the color she was told to dye it, and wore the make up that was purchased for her. And she learned to smile, to flirt, to give the customers the experience they had paid for—it was either that or receive a beating or a "tune up" with the hanger.

On Christmas Eve, a taxi delivered her to a hotel room. A member of a visiting club was in town and had contacted Doug for some company for the evening. Jackie was given tightfitting pedal pushers and five-inch heels to accentuate her legs. A tightfitting blouse completed the ensemble. One of the other girls did her hair and, with the addition of bright lipstick, blue eye shadow, and roughed cheeks, she could have passed for twenty-four on any street corner in town. She tried to explain to Doug that she was having her menstrual period at the time but, because she'd used that excuse before, he ignored her pleas and ordered the taxi.

Jackie knocked on the door of the room. The bolt slid back from the inside and she slipped into the room. The "date" was waiting for her, and with no preliminaries other than to slip on a condom, he ordered her to undress. She did so, explaining as best she could that she was menstruating and that she had tried to tell Doug that he should have sent over one of the other girls.

Used to the manipulations and excuses of prostitutes, the man reached between her legs and checked. When he had satisfied himself that yes, she was having her period, he laughed. "That son of a bitch Doug—he set me up! Well, little lady, the joke's on him. I told him I wanted some company for tonight and you're the designated Ho. Roll over."

Jackie, realizing what he intended to do, fought and tried to reach the door. He reached her before she could unhook the safety chain and pulled her back to the bed. Roughly rolling her over on her stomach, he raped her anally.

The night was an eternity of pain and humiliation for Jackie. She had been beaten in the past, and had endured many degrading and debasing acts forced upon her, but never had she felt so worthless.

As the early morning sun pushed its way through the eighth story window of the room, she pulled herself away from the sleeping man and gathered her clothes. She quietly slipped them on, unlocked the door and left the room.

It was early Christmas morning. As she walked through the lobby of the hotel, she saw all around her the tinsel and glitter of the holiday season. A decorated evergreen tree stood majestically in the center of the foyer. Gaily wrapped boxes were scattered under the tree and, although she knew they were only empty boxes decorated to look like presents, she thought how much they looked like those she'd received from her parents last year. A couch and chair were placed strategically near the entrance to the restaurant, just across the carpet from the reception desk. She couldn't hold herself together any longer and collapsed on the chair and cried.

"Can I help you, Miss?" The kind voice forced her to look up into the gentle face of the night manager. He was just going off shift and had spotted the young girl coming out of the elevator. He had kept an eye on her as she viewed the tree and the joyful trappings and grew concerned when she sat down and cried. "Why don't you phone your folks and let them know where you are. I'm sure they would welcome you back for Christmas."

His instinctive comments brought forth another torrent of tears as Jackie nodded numbly. He helped her to her feet and over to the house phone on the wall. He watched as she dialed a number from memory.

"Hello Mom—it's me."

The hotel employee could not hear the rest of the conversation as she turned her back on him and spoke quietly into the telephone. The conversation was short and the look on her face as she placed the receiver back onto the hook was one of shocked disbelief. "They don't want me home," she whispered through fresh tears.

She looked at the older man questioningly. "They said I'd caused them all sorts of embarrassment and that I couldn't just waltz back into their life whenever I felt like it. I can't go home." She turned, numb, and walked out the front door and climbed into an idling cab.

As the taxi left the lot with Jackie in the back, the customer in the room was reaching for the phone. He dialed Doug's cell phone number, getting him out of bed. The conversation was brief. Although there was surface humor over the unexpected situation of Jackie's condition, there was also no doubt about the irritation felt by the out of town customer who felt cheated by being unable to enjoy himself to the fullest. Doug promised suitable compensation.

Doug rolled away from Cindy as he put the phone back onto the night stand. "That little ho! She's getting to be more trouble than she's worth! This is about the fifteenth time she's ticked off one of the customers. This time she's not going to get away with it!"

He sorted through a pile of dirty clothes on the floor, located his jeans and walked to the front room. Barefooted, he was pacing the floor as the cab pulled to the curb outside the house and Jackie emerged. She walked up to the side door of the house and entered.

As she closed the door behind her, she spotted Doug standing in the room. Before she could utter a word, Doug's voice drove her back. "What the fuck are you trying to do? It's Christmas morning and I get woke up by a guy who paid me good money for you. He's pissed off because you wouldn't give him a proper piece of ass. Now what's with you? Do I have to get the wire and teach you another lesson? Tell me. What's with you?"

"That son-of-a-bitch raped me!" she yelled at her pimp. "I told you I was having my period and you didn't believe me! So he just raped me—like a dog!"

In two strides Doug was over her. As she cowered, he reached down and grabbed her hair. "Don't you ever yell at me. Ever!" Dragging her into the basement, he slapped her repeatedly across the face. "Don't you ever learn? Doesn't it ever sink in that you're a whore? When are you going to learn that you are nothing! You do what I tell you, when I tell you and how I tell you. You dissed me in front of my customers just one too many times. I gave you plenty of opportunity to learn to be a good ho, but no-o-o! You had to do it your own way. This time you're going to get a lesson that will stay with you forever!"

He dragged her across the cement floor. Taking a length of rope from a workbench in the corner, he tied her hands and looped the rope over the ceiling beam. He stuffed an oily rag into her mouth when she started to scream.

Jackie tried to kick and fight, but her plight didn't allow her to do much more than put up token resistance. Doug unsheathed a lock-blade knife from his belt, flicked it open and inserted the blade between the waistband of her slacks and her stomach. With a tug on the blade, the fabric tore loose. With a few more cuts, the pants lay in tatters at her feet.

"So, you think a little blood excuses you from having to work, do ya? Well maybe you just need to have it plugged up for awhile!" Saying this, he grabbed a broom, breaking the bristles off the end. He held the splintered end in front of Jackie's eyes. As she stared at the wood, he stepped back and viciously kicked her between the legs. Cindy, standing at the top of the stairs to the basement, could hear Jackie's pelvic bones crush under the force of the blow. Using his fists, his feet and the broken broom stick, the brutal punishment continued for half an hour. Jackie received a devastating beating, more violent than Cindy had ever witnessed. When he finished, he undid the rope and Jackie collapsed unconscious to the floor. Doug yelled to Cindy.

"Get down here and clean her up. I want her dressed and ready for work in fifteen minutes. Do you understand?" Cindy nodded. Fear motivated her to work quickly. Although she was Doug's main bitch, she knew that even she was not immune from his discipline.

She quickly slipped a skirt over Jackie's thighs and added a light blouse. As the young girl regained consciousness, she whispered quickly and urgently to her. "Get up and get going. He wants you working again in a few minutes. You *have* to do it! When you get a chance, run to a police car, a fire hall or anywhere you can! You've got to make it, 'cause if you don't, I think Doug will kill you. Can you do that?" Jackie nodded.

The two girls slowly made their way up the steps, Cindy holding the younger girl up by her armpits, practically forcing her to mount each step.

When they reached the kitchen, Doug was on the telephone to the customer who had anally raped Jackie. He hung up and turned to the girls.

"The guy you were with last night is coming by. You owe him a free one for the way you treated him. I have to go downtown too, so when he comes, I'll ride as far as the hotel. This time, you better not diss me. I've just about had enough of your shit."

Cindy had turned the radio on low, the dial tuned to a country station. As the customer pulled up in front of the bungalow and the two people left the home—master and slave. They closed the door on the gentle strains of *Silent Night*.

Three days after the celebration of the birth of Christ, a welder working on an industrial project, went to throw some scrap iron into a garbage bin. It bounced against the side and toppled over the back. When he went to recover the junk, he found the battered body of a young girl. There was speculation, never proven, that Jackie had followed Cindy's advice and tried to reach the police. The location of her body, and the condition of the corpse, indicated that she had put up a valiant fight.

In the ensuing investigations, both Doug and the customer were arrested. Cindy spoke to the investigating officers, telling them, that she was in fear of her life. She refused to testify and there were no other witnesses. Both men swore they had been together the entire morning. A search of Doug's basement revealed the presence of the rope, the oily rag, a quantity of blood, and a tiny gold locket on a broken chain.

One year later, Cindy disappeared. Doug has a new main now and his stable has expanded—all young girls who have dabbled in drugs and are attempting to repay their debts.

5

Sukan

I miss you in the heart.

S HE pushed her hair back from her forehead. It had been a long and fruitless day and she was tired. She wasn't used to the constant bustle of the street and, although her nervousness had passed some time ago, she admitted to herself that she still wasn't as comfortable as she should be down here near the waterfront. In her hands, she held a spiral notebook in which she had filled the right side of each page with double-spaced writing. This was how she'd been taught. Her notes almost filled the book but she was no closer to solving the enigma now than she had been a month ago.

The young social work student was undertaking "street work"—completing her practicum requirements. It had been her task to assess and complete a thesis on the growing problem of juvenile sex trade workers in Toronto. During daily outings, she spoke to dozens of street people: evaluating, assessing, reporting and compiling the numerous bits of information concerning children who, for one reason or another, became permanent residents of the downtown core. Recently she came across a disturbing piece of information from one of her street contacts, and as she attempted to track down and confirm the information's validity, she grew increasingly frustrated and angry.

At every turn she was told that the story was a fabrication, a lie, the output of someone's overactive imagination. Her fellow social workers, the various agencies, even the police, discounted the material that had been passed along to her. Now, having come across another piece of the puzzle, she was being very cautious. As a student, with her third year coming up, she didn't want to appear to be an alarmist or a gullible novice, so her second set of inquiries were meticulous—bordering on paranoia.

She had resisted making the phone call, although the number had been given to her as a contact. Now, she felt she had no alternative.

When someone answered the telephone, she spoke quietly. "Hello Coyote? This is the student. I wonder if I could meet you somewhere? I have some information I'd like to check out with you." She paused as the individual at the other end of the line *made a comment. She felt like some character in a "B" movie, but this was the only way she could think of to connect with someone who just might be able to confirm her information.*

After agreeing on a time and location, she set the phone back in the cradle and left the booth. She was nervous about meeting the man, having heard of his reputation from several of her contacts. Their comments hadn't been favorable, but if anyone knew the answers to some very puzzling questions, it would be him. Whether or not he would share his information was very much in doubt, but at least she had to make the effort.

"It's becoming more and more like some spy script," she thought as she parked her car in a city lot on Yonge Street. "I really shouldn't be doing this—I'm way out of my depth here. No one knows where I am, what I'm doing,—Hell I don't know what I'm doing! I'm waiting for a man I've never met, one who plays both ends against the middle as long as there's money involved." Her breath caught as a tap came on the passenger window. She looked into the face of the man she had phoned. She leaned over and lifted the lock. He swung open the passenger door, climbed in and quickly pulled it closed, extinguishing the interior light.

Two hours passed as the two sat in the darkened lot, the student asking questions and Coyote providing information. The young social worker was surprised at the amount of general street information he was willing to part with. He was reluctant, however, to reveal much about the topic of interest to her.

She tried to jot down some notes, but when she flipped open her notebook and turned on the overhead light, his violent outburst of colorful profanity quickly convinced her that he was as nervous about the topic as she was. Although she never asked why he was sharing the information with her, she came to believe that, in some fashion, this situation disturbed him as well. She could understand, with his extensive criminal background, why he could not go to the police, so maybe this was his way of revealing information while still remaining anonymous. This became clear when he told her directly that if she ever tried to use his name as a source she would "live to regret it."

With that threat, he left the car. It was now up to her. Going from one contact to another, speaking to street people and picking up rumors, her investigation took shape.

By the fall, she gathered together her notes and completed a detailed and shocking indictment. The police officer to whom she passed the report was intrigued by her notes. Turning the pages, one by one, the story unfolded before him.

• • •

Life was tough for the hill people of central Cambodia, but for eight year old Sukan, it was particularly difficult. Today she had not eaten at all and yesterday she only received a small amount of rice. Returning from gathering firewood in the barren hills above the town, her stomach growled with hunger. The dusty street of the village was populated by scrawny goats, chickens, and children. She was lonely. She was now the oldest girl in the village, many of her friends having left home to be hostesses or dancers in Thailand. Sukan missed them greatly. Her father, Tai Lin, and mother, Chin Son, had resisted earlier offers from the men who had taken her friends away, but she knew in her heart that it was only a matter of time before she too, would have to leave.

The missionary's school had closed during the last monsoon season and never reopened. Home full-time, her chores were limited to gathering the few eggs which were laid by the chickens owned by her father and helping her mother with simple tasks around the house. The few vegetables her mother planted near the side of their shack failed to thrive. This was the third year in a row that the garden was a failure. Tai Lin had been able to keep the family intact by earning a little money working at backbreaking labor in the valley. But his employer, a rubber plantation owner, had mechanized much of the work and this had thrown him out of a job. They never had much, but now the family was on the verge of starvation.

Cambodia is a country shrouded in mystery. An ancient civilization, the people live much as they have done for thousands of years. When she was a little girl, Tai Lin would tell Sukan the stories of his youth—when every family had a plot of land to grow their food, when there was peace in the countryside, and the King was kind. He would lull her to sleep with the stories of the greatness of their native country and how one time he had even seen the Crown Prince. But then the fighting came. The war in the mid 1970s and the overthrow of the government by the Khmer Rouge Communists changed the face of the nation. Now a land that was once prosperous was in shambles. With a population of over ten million compressed into an area smaller than the state of Oklahoma, the prospect of gaining some sort of employment to enable Tai Lin to feed his family was bleak indeed. Something would have to be done and it was this knowledge that caused the sadness in Sukan.

Chickens scattered, goats bleated, and the dust swirled, and a blowing horn trumpeted the arrival of a big touring sedan. It was cause for excitement, for the same sedan had been to the settlement before and on each occasion it had left with several young girls from the village. The families of the girls always received money, sometimes enough to allow them to live normally for the following year. Of those who left, Sukan could not remember any returning. This time, the car came to a halt in front of Sukan's hut.

Two men alighted from the vehicle. The taller one, opening the passenger door, was dressed in western attire with a suit and tie. The driver wore a high-collar jacket, fashionable during the days of the communists. The villagers watched as the tall man opened the rear door and spoke to the passengers—two girls. He motioned them out of the car, pointing to a fence on the far side of the roadway. They giggled, then ran behind the pickets. He waited for their return, then closed the door behind them. They appeared well-taken care of; their faces were scrubbed, each had on a new dress and there were no constraints holding them to the strangers. The driver and passenger walked to the front of Sukan's hut.

"Hello Tai Lin. Are you ready to talk now?" asked the taller man. Tai Lin nodded and indicated several low stools. Chin Son did not join the gathering, preferring to leave the business at hand to the men. She collected the younger children and shooed them down the street. Only Sukan was allowed to remain; she was instructed to go inside and wash.

Tai Lin had been expecting the men for some time. He sat back on his heels and considered their proposal. The little girl could not hear the entire conversation, but the occasional words that floated through the thin walls of the hut caused her some concern. She wanted to be a part of the discussion, but respect for her father prevented her from being present. She knew from experience that she was the topic of conversation and this knowledge both excited and worried her. It appeared that she was going to be able to leave this dusty village for adventure in a far off place. That was the excitement—the worry was that she didn't know where she would be going.

She was called to the front of the home by her father. Opening the door she saw that the men were now standing, their negotiations complete. Although Tai Lin knew he would never see his eldest daughter again, he felt that whatever lay before young Sukan would be better than remaining in the village and starving. The payment was enough to last them a year, perhaps until the crops got better. This was enough of an incentive to assuage his conscience and bury his concerns. After all, he had his wife, his mother-in-law and three other children to provide for, didn't he? And besides, the men promised that Sukan would be able to come back each year, and bring home the money she had made as an entertainer.

Sukan had thoroughly washed herself while she was waiting and, after concluding the transactions, one of the men took a small package from the trunk of the car and handed it to her. "Go and put these on," he commanded in a deceptively gentle voice. "You have to look nice from now on." Sukan took the package and returned to her corner of the house.

Hidden behind a blanket suspended from the ceiling, she unwrapped the package. Inside were bright new clothes: a skirt, a pure white blouse, stockings, and sandals. Wrapped in paper were several candy bars, nuts, and a variety of sweetmeats. She never in her short life had such delicious things given to her. If this was how her future was to be, maybe it wouldn't be so bad. Maybe she shouldn't worry at all. Delighted with her new clothes, she tossed her old ones aside, and slipped into the colorful new ones. She broke a small piece from one of the candy bars and rolled it around in her mouth. The remaining treats she stuffed into a small bag and hid under her skirt.

Brushing the curtain aside, she walked back into the sunshine, twirling in circles as she showed her new outfit to her father. Tai Lin smiled sadly as he watched his daughter. The tall passenger took out a camera and, after summoning the entire family back to the front of the hut, posed them for a picture. He promised to send a copy to the parents so they could remember their daughter until she returned.

Chin Son stood beside her husband as Sukan was escorted to the car. Her Grandmother remained where she had been sitting, not giving any notice to Sukan's pending departure. The three younger children waved excitedly as the door was closed behind Sukan and the car was put in gear.

It was late afternoon by the time the deal had been concluded and the two men were anxious to make up some time. There was one more stop to make, one more girl to be picked up. As the three girls chatted in the rear seat, the big car climbed higher into the hills. The sun was low on the western horizon as the fourth young child was fitted into the rear seat and the car headed towards the neighboring country of Thailand.

The girls quickly became friends. This was the first time that any of them had been away from their villages and they excitedly pointed out new discoveries to one another. Night had fallen by the time the car stopped at the border crossing. The girls had been asleep for several hours, one leaning against the other, when the low conversation awoke them. A flashlight, beamed into the back of the car, momentarily blinded the girls. They raised their hands to cover their eyes. The person at the other end of the beam spoke quietly to the driver. Money was passed to the guard, and the car continued through the checkpoint and down the highway. Once safely inside Thailand, the men stopped the car at a larger village. This time however, it was not to pick up children, but to rest. They pulled into an alley beside a travelers' lodging.

The four girls were given food and allowed to relieve themselves, and then they were placed in a room with one large mattress on the floor. Tired from the excitement of the past twenty-four hours, they fell into a deep peaceful sleep. They had no thought of trying to escape—they did not even know that the door had been bolted from the outside.

They were shaken awake by the tall man in the western suit. The girls were taken to a small bath house at the rear of the inn and were told to wash thoroughly. They splashed and chatted, excitement growing as the adventure unfolded. When they completed their toiletries, they were toweled dry and each was given a gown of raw silk and taken back to the room. No sooner had they entered than an older woman pushed open the door. She set a large suitcase on the floor and instructed each of the girls in turn to hop up on a tall stool.

The lady worked with the men who traveled the hilly roads of Cambodia, searching out fresh young girls for the demanding and discriminating buyers in Thailand. She was entrusted with the task of "dressing up the merchandise" to ensure the highest price possible was bid for the children.

She completed the work on each youngster and, as they were let down from the stool, she surveyed her handiwork. The girls had been scrubbed clean. Minor blemishes in the skin had been camouflaged with make up and fresh flowers woven into their hair. The four girls, with their olive complexion, diminutive stature, and glistening black locks, stood in stark contrast to the squalor and poverty outside. They were as marketable a commodity as the woman could create.

The girls were coached on how to walk and carry themselves. They were cautioned against any talking unless the master asked them a question, and even then they were to restrict their answers to "yes sir," or "no sir." It was impressed on each of them that their performance would have a direct bearing on where they would go. The better they moved and presented themselves—the better their price. The better the price, the more exotic and exciting their ultimate destination would be. All four were determined to excel.

Finally, the moment arrived. They were given final instructions and taken to a small room. Three men were present. One was the tall passenger from the car that had picked them up from their villages. The other two were strangers to the girls, but from the conversations carried out between the adults, they were not strangers to each other.

It was hard work. First the girls were paraded in front of the men, turning, preening, and evoking as provocative a manner as they could. There was a competitive atmosphere among the girls, as each tried to outdo the other. They were told to dance, to run, to jump up and down, to stand, first on one foot, then the other.

The woman told each girl to shed her robe and stand naked in front of the men. At first the youngsters were embarrassed by the request, but were reassured that it was only to determine the status of their health. They were told that if they were not healthy, the men may not choose any of them, and they would have to go back to their villages. This caused the girls to try harder, and they readily shed their clothes and walked back into the room.

There was a repetition of earlier requests. The girls were told to move, jump and stand in specific positions. After deliberating between themselves, the men made their choices. Only two would be selected: Sukan and Mai Ling. No mention was made of what would happen to the others.

The following two weeks were a blur of activity. The woman who had dressed them and applied their makeup was their constant companion. She taught them how to walk with grace, how to speak a few words in English, how to lower their eyes when a man spoke to them. During fourteen days, they were introduced to a young couple who, they were told, were going to take them to a faraway country where they would become actresses and make a lot of money to help their families at home. They learned to refer to the couple as their "parents," and to memorize new names and backgrounds in case a policeman asked them questions.

They were cautioned that all policemen were their enemies and would kill them if they found out that they were not the real children of the couple who were working with them. The belief that they would be rich, coupled with the fear that they would be killed if caught, made them study their roles with intensity and dedication. They would not fail!

On the day they were to leave, they were once again dressed in silk gowns. A final check was made by the men who, for the hundredth time it seemed, questioned them on their new backgrounds, parents, and destination. The girls' responses were given flawlessly—they passed with honors.

After such an intensive schooling, the excitement building up to the big moment and the endless rehearsing, the actual event was anticlimactic. As they departed the airport at Bangkok, the customs officers spent only moments examining their passports. Sailing far above the clouds, the girls' spirits were conflicted between the wonders of flight and home sickness for the families they left behind.

Their arrival at the Pearson International Airport in Toronto caused a few anxious moments. The Immigration Officer handling their entry cast a sharp and experienced eye over the "family" entering the secure area. The documents were presented by the "father" and the official took an uncomfortable length of time examining their credentials. He motioned the two adults to a nearby bench and spoke to the two young girls. Mai

Ling scuffed her shoes and refused to raise her eyes. She would not answer any of the questions put to her. The uniformed officer accepted her demeanor as shy and reserved. He then stooped down and questioned Sukan. He was charmed by her grace and good manners when she smiled and answered, "Yes sir!" to each and every question he posed.

He did not know any of the Asian languages. Had he any familiarity with them, he would have been able to detect the differences between the Thai language spoken by the adults in the group and the Khmer language spoken by the two young girls. It was unfortunate, not for him, but for the two girls, who had this one opportunity to break free of their captors. Had they done so, they would have been able to avoid a life that was to take some sinister turns.

For now, the girls had no sense that the future would be anything but one long play time. To them, this was what dreams were made of. They were excited as only children can be on this, the single most exciting adventure of their young lives. From the time they had left their villages, they had been pampered, had their every wish fulfilled. In the three weeks since they vacated their dusty homes and hopped into the back seat of that big old car, they ate better food, dressed in better clothes, slept longer and received better treatment than they had ever experienced in their entire lives.

Eventually, the paperwork was approved, their baggage collected, and the foursome left the secure area. The noise and bustle of the airport was confusing and they wandered around for a time, searching for the exit where they would be making their next connection. Finally, after several dead end passages, they located the designated pick up location. This time, it was a white man who entered their lives. There had been no phone calls, no letters exchanged—nothing that could be intercepted by the authorities. The man had been alerted to their arrival by a message delivered to him earlier that day. He was only a courier, paid by others still deeper in the shadows, to locate and transport his assigned cargo from the point of entry to a safe house.

It was early evening when the odd assortment of associates in the courier's van arrived at the residence. Located in a quiet residential neighborhood, there was little to differentiate the dwelling from the others in the area. The van pulled into an open front-drive garage, and after the overhead door had closed, the passengers alighted.

The entrance to the home was from inside the garage. The girls happily skipped up the three steps to the door and, when the courier driver opened it, burst inside with delight. This was to be their new home! They had never seen such luxury. Shiny kitchen fixtures, an indoor bathroom, and carpet throughout the entire house were the first sights that greeted their eyes. The girls ran from room to room, exclaiming excitedly over the many wonders. They played with the light switches and flushed the toilet a dozen times, fascinated with the flow of fresh water.

They darted down the hallway, abruptly coming to a halt when they ran into the man who had posed as their father throughout the trip. He gripped each by the upper arm, shoving them rudely along the hall into the kitchen. Pulling out two chairs, he shoved them down onto the seats. "Stay there," he commanded. Gone was his benevolent demeanor of the past two weeks—things had started to change.

● ● ●

The policeman finished reading the notes. It could be innocent, he thought, but on the other hand, maybe not. He dialed the number left by the student and arranged a meeting for the following day.

The two met over coffee and the detective questioned her for several hours. He went over the notes in detail, examining each piece of information, clarifying vague references, making his own set of notes. In the end though, he gleaned little more than she had recorded. Her notes were as complete as any trained investigator's: dates, facts, figures, and observations—all were meticulously registered. Questioned about her conversation with "Coyote," she was initially reluctant to reveal her source, but his obvious concern justified a change of mind. She told him what little information she had on this dim character. She was not able to give an address but the phone number she had used to make contact with Coyote was willingly offered. The detective laid a five dollar bill on the table, said, "My treat," thanked her and left.

The police investigation began immediately. The detective shared the data with his partner and, although the details were now eight weeks old, they pursued the vague and tenuous leads. Some had been gleaned from the worker's notes, others were cultivated from their own sources. Within a few hours of leaving the restaurant, "Coyote" had been identified. He was a low-level drug dealer, a part time bouncer, and general petty crook, who lived a violent life, picking up whatever short-term jobs came his way. Now to find him. The phone number was checked through the telephone company—listed to a pay phone in a bar on Spadina Avenue. From there it was a simple matter of sitting in the bar, having a quiet beer and waiting for the arrival of their quarry.

Coyote could have been the creator of the saying that "there is no loyalty among thieves." It did not take much pressure for him to tell the officers his role in transporting new arrivals from the airport to the safe house. The fact that he had several outstanding warrants for his arrest served a useful purpose as well—no doubt aiding in refreshing his memory. The information he turned over to the police was quickly checked and determined to be valid. The two detectives dropped their informant back where they found him and he returned to his favorite exercise—sitting in the bar. They drove back to their downtown office to spend some time making sense of their notes and to sort through the data. After discussing the matter with their immediate superior, it was decided that the proper investigative authority was the Department of Immigration. The two organizations had worked together on prior occasions, so the teaming of agencies was not a problem and a quick plan of action was drawn up. The two teams met at a predetermined location, several blocks from the target address.

Because of the nature of the crime, "Unlawful Entry to Canada," a search warrant was not required. The authority, given to the officers by the Immigration Act, was sufficient for them to forcibly enter the home, if required. It was.

With two officers at the front of the house and two at the rear, they announced their presence and demanded entry. When no response was received, the door was forced open. A quick search revealed that although there were signs of recent occupancy, it was now empty. The birds had flown the nest.

The police officers turned over their notes to the Senior Immigration Officer. There was no indication of anything wrong other than the fact that, with thousands of illegal immigrants filtering through Canada's borders, four more could now be added to the list. That theory itself was not even confirmed; they only had the word of a petty thief that these people were in the country unlawfully. Standing outside the home, the officers discussed the situation. The case was left in the hands of Immigration and the file was marked "For Information Only" and promptly shelved along with hundreds of other reports in the understaffed office. The social work student was advised of the investigation's conclusion and she was thanked politely for her interest.

She continued the trail on her own.

The inquiries carried out by the young social work student went beyond those conducted by either the police or immigration authorities. She talked to neighbors on both sides of the modern bungalow, then those across the street. She spoke to the mailman, examined utility records, checked the land titles office for a record of ownership; in fact, she did some very superior investigative work.

Her unofficial evidence revealed that the house had been rented through a local real estate company. The management of the premises was through a property management firm who took deposits, arranged moving dates, and made sure the residence returned a profit to its owners. They had no knowledge of the individuals involved, other than that they seemed to travel a lot and always paid in cash and on time. The spokesperson for the management company informed the young woman that the rent had been paid for the next several months but he could not guess when the couple might return from their travels. It appeared, at least for now, that the trail was at a dead end. The young girls who had been brought illegally into the country had disappeared.

• • •

As the courier's van disappeared down the street, the two girls were bathed and put to bed in one of the bungalow's bedrooms. They were told, "Get a good sleep" because their "training" would start in the morning. They were informed that this training would have to be completed before they could become famous actresses.

When they awoke they were fed and ordered to clean up and prepare for the first part of their education. The woman, who also assumed the role of instructor, laid out suitable clothing for them. This time, in addition to the fine silk gowns they had worn in Thailand, there were other clothes. Tiny swimsuits, barely covering their prepubescent bodies, western-style jumpers, and tight denim jeans. Each girl had her hair combed and braided and a very light coating of make up was applied to their young faces. Both were then taken into the front room of the home. The room had also undergone changes—what had once been a comfortable living room was now a professional studio.

There were all sorts of electronic props in the room—lights, cameras on tripods, backdrops, and fake trees. Sukan was the first to have photographs taken. She was positioned in a number of provocative poses;

leaning against a tree, sitting cross-legged on the floor, standing in front of a painted waterfall. Time after time the light flashed as she was told to change positions. Hands on her hips, on her hair, on her thigh. "Turn this way! Look that way! Pout your lips! Lift your hair!" Orders were given and obeyed. The other girl had similar pictures taken and then their outfits were changed, this time into innocent "school girl" clothes which emphasized their tender ages. The backdrops and props were rearranged and another series of photographs were taken. The session was long and difficult. If the girls did not move quickly enough they were yelled at and pushed roughly. In spite of the harshness of the adults, the two girls treated the photo sessions as yet another step in their budding careers as entertainers. Wearing the tiny swimsuits, little girl dresses, and even when they had to undress completely to be photographed nude, the girls experienced conflicting emotions, ranging from apprehension to excitement.

The photo session lasted until noon. They were given a short break, then told to dress once more in the silk gowns.

In the early afternoon, the two girls were taken from the house and paraded through numerous gatherings, populated exclusively by men. By supper time, they had been returned to the safe house.

Sukan and her friend were exhausted. The day's activity had started early and the endless demands on their time was taking its toll. They nodded their way through a quick supper and wandered back to their room. As the streetlights flickered on, men came to the home. Some came alone, others came in groups of two or three, but all entered through the same garage entrance. Each was greeted at the door and shown into the living area. By mid evening, a dozen men, all contacts from earlier in the afternoon, were seated, each with a drink in hand. The girls were brought out, and once again, paraded before the men.

The tall male, who was their constant companion, clapped his hands and gained the attention of the group. He spoke for several minutes, joking with several of the men and chiding a few who shook their heads. Within minutes, money had been collected from each man and pocketed by the organizer. Two men removed sizable rolls of money from their pockets and this also was passed along. The two high rollers were to be given the honor of deflowering the two virgin children seated on stools near the wall.

The youngsters were taken to separate bedrooms in the rear of the home and, after being robbed of their childhood by the two wealthiest men, the little girls were subjected to a series of rapes lasting through the night. One man would complete his act and another would take his place, the first returning to the living room to continue his conversation with the others, and perhaps to refresh his drink. The sun rose in the morning, signaling the dawning of a new and unspoiled day. Inside the home, the girls were also facing a new day. The youngsters were no longer the happy children of Cambodia, but rather victims of one of the most horrific experiences that could befall a child. Finally they were allowed to fall into an exhausted sleep.

When they awoke several hours later the men had gone and only the two "parents" remained. Both girls were taken from their rooms to the kitchen and were again given food and water.

These were not the first young girls the couple had worked with and they were masters at their craft. They showered the girls with affection, feeding them treats and stroking their hair. This was called "dogging" them, and like a dog who has been kicked and wants affection, so too did the girls. The adults were there to supply it. When they attempted to speak, they were slapped and told that they were no longer going to be entertainers, but prostitutes because they didn't measure up to the standards that had been expected of them. They were not pretty enough, not exotic enough for the North Americans. They were then told that they would have to help earn money so that they could return to their homes.

The children were reminded of their relatives back in the hills of Cambodia and each was shown the picture that had been taken on the day of their departure. As they viewed the photos and remembered their families, both cried deep racking sobs. That same afternoon the man who had picked them up at the airport returned. Once again he drove into the garage and closed the doors. The four climbed into the van, the overhead door was opened, and the group left the house, never to return. Within days the empty house was raided.

● ● ●

The young social work student concluded her notes for the evening. All leads had been exhausted. It appeared that the two girls had disappeared into thin air. The house was vacant and—for now—the trail was cold.

She put down her pen. Had she forgotten anything, any detail, no matter how small? Had she interviewed everyone? Was there someone else she should contact? She returned to the suburban neighborhood. Having some time before she was to return to classes for the next semester, she once again knocked on doors throughout the area.

Knowing from her experiences that there was a busybody in every community, one who made it their mission to know everything going on throughout a district, she began to enlarge the scope of her inquiries. She rang the doorbells of over fifty homes in her first effort but this time she was looking for one particularly nosy individual. She finally found such a person and obtained a description of the van, as well as the first three digits of the license number. She phoned and demanded an appointment with the authorities.

The numbers were run through the Department of Motor Vehicles computer and a match-up was made to a registered vehicle, similar to the van described by the nosy resident. The Immigration Officers completed the necessary documentation and passed along the information to Customs. The customs officials, processing it as a routine request from a partner agency, entered the data on their computer as a B.O.L.F. (Be On Lookout For) at all border crossings. Within twenty-four hours it registered a "hit" at Niagara Falls, Ontario. The van was not trying to leave Canada for the United States, but rather returning to Canada from the United States. There was only one person on board, a scruffy white male. He was taken into custody for questioning by the Immigration Officers. He had run afoul of them before and was willing to part with what little information he knew.

• • •

The two girls were terrified as they approached the Canada/United States border crossing at Niagara Falls. It was not the uniformed officials they were afraid of, but their captors. A few blocks before the white customs house, the driver of the van pulled to the side of the road. The two adults seated in the rear with the youngsters told them, in chilling detail, what lay in store for them should they alert the officials at the border station. The girls nodded their understanding and curled up on the rear seat, pretending to be asleep.

As the van fell into the rear of a long line of cars awaiting inspection, the driver went over, once again, the roles they would play. He would pose as a hired driver who was returning them to Detroit. The two Asians had left their car in Windsor, Ontario for repairs after it had broken down. Passports were examined—new ones, showing U.S. citizenship—questions and answers were rehearsed and expressions fixed.

Like the border crossing from Cambodia to Thailand and the entrance to Pearson International Airport in Toronto, this too went unhindered. The group were not novices at this game and the documents they presented were as foolproof as any legitimate credential. In fact, they were legitimate. From a source in the United States, their visas were actual government issue. Only the pictures had to be altered and this was a minor operation. To all appearances, the group had every right to enter the United States.

The group drove the remaining distance to the outskirts of New York City, stopping only long enough for gasoline and bathroom breaks. The four were dropped off at a second safe house, this time located in an apartment over a strip club. The driver didn't want to hang around and, as soon as his passengers entered the building, he headed back to Canada and safety.

At this house, the girls did not run from room to room squealing in delight. This time they knew that the life they had expected was not to be theirs. They also knew that the chances of ever seeing their families again were slim. In fact, as they huddled together in yet another locked room, they realized that the likelihood was nonexistent.

Music and the sound of voices came from the club downstairs as the girls were taken from their darkened compartment and brought into the brightly-lit front room. The man who had by now been their constant companion since Cambodia, the one they had been taught to call "father," stood in front of them.

"You are going to be leaving me tonight. There are men downstairs— no, they are not here for sex—they are here to take you to a new place. You have both been very good and I want you to be good for just another hour. You must follow my instructions exactly. Remember, if you do not do as I tell you, I know where your families live and I will have them killed. Do you understand?"

The girls nodded.

"Okay. We're going downstairs. I want you to listen to everything I say and do everything I tell you to do. You must not make any mistakes. This is important for you. Depending on how well you do, you can live a life of riches, or have a miserable life. It is all your responsibility. I want you to smile all the time and do as I say." Not waiting for a reply, he pushed the two youngsters ahead of him towards the back staircase leading to the rooms below.

As they descended the stairs, the noise grew louder. At the bottom landing the man stopped them and told them to remove all their clothes. On their right shoulder he wrote a number with a black felt tip pen, then herded them into a large room behind the stage normally assigned to the strippers for their relaxation between dances. As they entered, they were confronted by a room jammed full of girls their own age, all naked, and all with numbers written on their right shoulders. Tonight there were no strippers, the girls themselves were the focus of the evening. Sukan looked around her and counted nineteen others, some her own age, some slightly older. None appeared to be over ten years old. She clung to her friend in terror.

The door opened briefly, as an overweight white man stuck his head in the door and asked if everyone was ready. The two adults guarding the door nodded. The door closed and the fat man climbed onto the stage. He looked out into the audience. Tonight there was a nice mix of customers. Some blacks, some whites, some Asians and some from the Middle East. All were men, all were wealthy, and all came to purchase a product. They were not here to buy a hour or so of a girl's time, to engage in passionless sex. They were here tonight to buy the children—body and soul.

Spotlights flooded the stage as the announcer adjusted the microphone.

One by one the girls paraded onto the stage. The announcer, looking at a paper in his hand, revealed the details of each child as she moved through the spotlight. Their names, their ages, their backgrounds. He added that they had all been trained in the oriental arts of sex, describing in detail, embellishing with great delight, the abilities of the child prostitutes he was auctioning to the men seated below.

With jokes and an auctioneer's patter, he worked the crowd with expert skill. The girls were reminded to smile and ordered to turn, to jump, to bend over, and to strike alluring poses. The audience was silent. They weren't here for entertainment, but to purchase new flesh for their demanding clients scattered throughout the northeastern United States.

As the last order was issued, the girls were herded off the stage and back to the large room. From then on they were taken out one by one, to be auctioned off. The customers received an extensive overview of the available merchandise and now the bidding began in earnest. Some could only afford one girl and, in those instances, she did not return to the room. Other men had deeper pockets and bid on several. When a new owner had selected two or more, they were taken back to the room their numbers recorded and they were dressed in new clothes. The girls awaited their fate with terror.

Sukan, because of her tender age and exquisite beauty, was reserved for the end. She felt that if she could sufficiently impress the richest man there, she would receive special consideration when he took her from the club and to her next assignment. Once again, she was determined to excel.

When her number was called, she hopped onto the stage and skipped across it. Although her heart was aching, she smiled, danced, twisted and turned, doing everything in her limited power to impress the men who were placing bids on her very life. The bidding was spirited.

Finally the auctioneer had winnowed the bidders down to two—both white males who thought that this particular find was a gold mine. The bids climbed higher and higher. The excitement of the calls from the gathering was felt by Sukan and she tried even harder. Spiraling, arching, bending, smiling—anything to increase her value. Finally the last bid was called. "Going once, going twice, sold!"

Sukan's eight year-old life was hawked for forty-two thousand dollars— the highest price ever paid for a prostitute at this site.

The new owner could expect up to ten years of work from the child. With an expected return of a thousand dollars a night, working six days a week, he stood to make the greatest profit of his career. True, Sukan's innocent beauty would one day fail and the prices for her services would go down. One day she would die. One day the man would return and Sukan would be replaced by another.

Rumors abounded about the auction, informants came forward with stale information, and children went missing. All investigations failed. The very horror of that night, and too many others like it, kept the auction so secretive that no one except a few initiates ever knew it happened.

• • •

The young social worker closed her notebook. Sukan was never found.

6

Christine

*How come the churches help the kids in Africa, but not us? How come they have
telethons for kids that have diseases, but not for those who have been raped dozens
of times? How come adults get upset about a dog that is tortured, but not about
kids that get beaten? How come, huh?*

FAMILY life for the Jamiesons was all they had ever hoped and planned
for. They had a beautiful daughter, commitment to each other, and
a family full of love. Throw in a pastoral setting, far from the
corruption of the city, and Norman Rockwell couldn't have painted a better
scene. Cam and his wife Alana had moved from the cramped quarters of
their city apartment to the open spaces of the Rocky Mountain foothills,
just months after the adoption of their little girl Christine. Only eight
days old when they signed the papers, Christine became the center of
their lives. The precocious blonde-haired, blue-eyed child completed their
feeling as a family, after years of being denied the joy of parenthood.

Cam left his job in the petroleum industry, taking a significant pay cut
to work as a draftsman for this rural county. Alana, feeling she wanted
time to be with their child, stepped out of the paid workforce to become
a full-time homemaker and mother. A new circle of friends formed, and
they became active in the local church and energetic participants in
community affairs. As Christine grew into a beautiful and talented girl,
they added singing lessons, highland dancing and Girl Guides to their
weekly list of "must do's."

Christine flourished with her parents' love and dedication. She became
an above average student, enjoyed a large measure of popularity, and was
the envy of every girl her age in the community of mainly white, blue
collar families.

Though, at age eleven, she was a little self-conscious when her figure
started to fill out, the reassurances of her mother convinced her that she
was just "more mature" than her friends and that she should be proud of
how she looked, not embarrassed.

The first sprinkle of snow fell, covering the hills in a blanket of early winter and bringing down a gentle backdrop on the Jamieson's annual Thanksgiving supper. The celebration rotated annually throughout the family and, this year's celebration would be held in the country. The turkey was in the oven, pies and cakes on the sideboard, sweet potatoes, creamed corn, and cranberry jelly were heaped in bowls along the center of the table. Cam's parents arrived by bus from their home a thousand miles to the south, and Alana's sister and her husband drove up to share in the celebrations. The family was excited, as this would be Aunt Kathy and Uncle George's first visit to the Jamieson home in almost six years. All the visitors planned to stay a few days after the holidays to visit and reminisce about old friends and good times past.

Christine idolized her Aunt Kathy. Vivacious and pretty, her aunt's bold manner impressed the young girl. There was no holding back when it came to speaking her mind and many of Aunt Kathy's outspoken comments bordered on the scandalous. The youngster was flattered when, after supper, her aunt singled her out for a "walk in the country." She felt so grown up, being drawn into the circle by her favorite relative.

The two slipped their feet into winter boots, drew warm coats around their shoulders and took a walk along the back trail towards the upper meadow. The leaves had fallen from the trees and the chill of the coming winter carried on the breeze from the north. Only when they entered the protective shelter of the tree line, halfway up the hill, did the cut of the wind diminish sufficiently for them to talk.

Kathy stopped for a moment to allow Christine to catch up. "So...how have you been doing this past year?" She let herself down onto a log, patting the bark beside her. Christine sat alongside, catching her breath from the climb.

"Not too bad, but it gets kind of boring sometimes—you know."

"But you do all sorts of things," her aunt countered, "things like Guides, dancing and sports! I'd think that would keep you plenty busy. How can you be bored?"

"Oh, you know. The weekends. I have to do the chores and stuff, and Mom and Dad just sit around. I wish you lived closer to us, then I could go over to your place and visit and stuff."

The two companions visited amicably, protected from the chilly wind coming down off the distant mountains. Aunt Kathy chatted with the young girl, revealing a portion of her own struggles and triumphs, sorrows, and joys. Christine reveled in the kinship they shared. "So how come I'm not like Mom and Dad?" she asked as the conversation turned to the topic of family traits. "I don't even look like them. I have blonde hair, they are both dark. I have blue eyes and Mom's are brown and Dad's are gray. Doesn't that seem strange to you Aunt Kathy?"

The older woman turned and looked at her companion. "Didn't your folks ever talk to you about things?"

"What do you mean?"

"About where you came from and everything?" Kathy knew she shouldn't be discussing these matters with Christine—her sister and brother-in-law should have by now—but now she'd started, she couldn't back away from pursuing the question. "Didn't they ever talk about when you were a baby?"

Christine shook her head, tears building in her eyes. "No. In fact, they never talk much about when I was a baby. I thought maybe they were embarrassed about me or something."

Kathy put her arm around the child. "Oh, honey no! Your folks aren't embarrassed about you at all. They love you—I was only asking if they had told you about your being adopted, that's all?"

"*Adopted!*" The word hit Christine like a sledgehammer. She turned and looked at her aunt. "Adopted? Are you telling me I was adopted? And they never told me? No wonder they're ashamed of me." She buried her face in her hands and started to sob.

"There, there, sweetheart. I didn't mean to make you cry. It's just that I thought by now you would've known everything. I thought your mom and dad would have told you." She patted Christine's hair, then hugged the child to her body. She spoke softly and soothingly to the youngster as she rocked her back and forth, quieting the sobs.

She shifted the conversation back onto safer ground. If Christine's mother was not going to explain everything to the child, then she certainly wasn't going to be the one. "Don't tell your folks I said anything, okay? They're probably just waiting for the best time to tell you. This can be just our secret—just you and me. Okay?" She felt Christine nod.

The news had hurt the girl deeply. She looked again into the face of her aunt. "Do you know who my real parents are?"

Her aunt remained still. "I think we've talked just about enough. I want this to be our secret. Now, give me a hug and we'll head on back. Grandpa and Grandma are real worry warts and your folks will be wondering where we've been." She stood and the girl slowly stood beside her.

"I'm glad you told me. It explains so much. I have to think about this for awhile...but I won't let on you told me." She smiled at her aunt through tears.

The two worked their way back through the growing dusk. With the wind now at their backs, the journey to the farmhouse passed quickly. The door opened as they clambered onto the porch. "Where have you two been?" Alana asked. "We've been getting worried, what with the darkness coming and the snow. We're just going to have some coffee and dessert. Hurry up and get out of those damp clothes and come have something hot to drink." She turned, motioning the two chilled walkers into the kitchen.

Christine was quiet during the rest of evening, her thoughts constantly returning to the revelation of her adoption. "Why hadn't they told me? Where are my real parents? Was there something wrong with me that my own mother would give me away?" She barely picked at the pumpkin pie her grandmother had baked and her hot chocolate grew cold on the table in front of her.

That holiday weekend would later be identified as the turning point in Christine's life. During the following year, Christine grew steadily more distant from the family. Increasingly, she stayed cooped up in her room, writing secretly in her diary, spending less and less time with her parents. Her marks dropped in school to the point where she was lucky if she received a passing grade—even in subjects she used to love. Her parents were worried.

When Christine dropped Girl Guides, then dancing, and then began associating with a rough crowd in town, Cam and Alana felt it was time to take action. They were not the type of parents who resorted to discipline each time they couldn't solve a problem. In fact, they always took care to fully evaluate a behavior or situation before acting. This time, however, they were baffled. They tried reasoning. They attempted to elicit from their daughter what it was that was troubling her. Each time they sat down for a talk, Christine shut them out, retreating inside herself to a place no one seemed able to reach.

Alana knocked on the door to Christine's room. "Sweetheart, may we come in?" There was a mumbled response. Cam turned the knob on the door and, accompanied by his wife, walked into the room. They decided to be blunt.

"Christine. We are really worried about you. For the last year you have shut us out. Your school work has suffered, you've dropped the things you enjoy. You're hanging around with a rough crowd. Do you have anything you want to say to us?" The young girl shook her head, turning back to the book she was reading.

Cam lost his temper and for the first time, he reacted to his daughter without thinking. He stomped across the room and ripped the book out of her hands. "Don't you turn away from us like that! We're your parents and we deserve an answer. You're fourteen years old and you *will* speak to us!" He stood over Christine, hands on his hips, waiting for her reply. What she said shocked him.

"You are *not* my parents! You lied to me! You never told me I was adopted! How come you never told me? Are you ashamed of me? No wonder you try to control me, just like everything else. That's why you moved out here to the sticks isn't it? So I would never find out about my real parents! If it wasn't for Aunt Kathy, I never would have found out!"

Alana and Cam were stunned. When words finally came, they were gentle, contrite. "Sweetheart, I'm sorry you had to find out from someone else. We were just waiting for the right time." There were tears in Cam's eyes.

"Yes...you are adopted. We couldn't have children of our own and we so wanted a little girl. You were that little girl. We did move to the country—partly because of you, but not because we were afraid you would find out, but only because we thought it would be better for all of us away from the city." Alana moved forward to reassure her daughter.

"Don't come near me!" Christine yelled, recoiling. "I don't want you to touch me! Just leave me alone!"

The two adults looked at each other. With a nod, they moved towards the door and turned. There was helplessness in Alana's voice, "Maybe we should have told you sooner, but there were good reasons not to. Give us a chance Christine, will you? We'll leave you alone tonight, but tomorrow we'll talk about it some more." They closed the door behind them and returned downstairs. They fully intended to speak to Christine the coming day, but many seasons would come and go before they would see her again.

Reconstruction of the events that followed were taken from Christine's diary and matched with information known to the parents, and the police.

• • •

The night of the confrontation, Christine slipped from her room, taking just a few clothes, and hitchhiked her way to the city. Arriving cold and alone, she may as well have had a sign reading *victim* stamped on her forehead. She'd squirreled away a bit of money over the years and, for the first few nights, she survived on this small nest egg. She booked herself a room in a cheap hotel, registering under a false name. She spent her few remaining dollars on some bakery buns and bologna.

By the fourth day she was broke. She had very few survival skills for these circumstances, but she was observant. In her walks through the various malls and centers, she noted a number of teenagers approach shoppers with a story and a request for small change. By the end of the day she would have to make up her mind. Either go home and accept her family for what it was, or survive as so many others seemed to be doing. She decided to try an approach.

"Excuse me. I'm really embarrassed about this, but I just got into town and I had my wallet stolen. Could you spare some change so I can phone my folks?"

The woman stopped. "Oh, you poor dear. Here." With that she opened her purse and took out a five dollar bill, passing it over to Christine. The girl was delighted. This was easy! Five bucks for five minutes work. She made up her mind. "No going back now! If she could do this a dozen times a day, she would have money for her room and food. She was learning how to survive."

She polished her lines, learning from each rebuff she received. The approach, the look, the feel for the situation, all had to be tailor-made for each potential target. Christine watched the more experienced panners, learning from them as she went along. By the third day of panhandling, she had established a rhythm and a pattern and moved "uptown" to pan money outside a large department store in the inner city. It was there she met Jamus.

For protection, Christine and several other young girls had teamed up—not so much to get money as to look out for one another. On this day, she was just pocketing her latest take when a voice alerted her. "Say girl, watcha all doin' down here." She looked up. The big smile of a young black man was the first thing she saw. She immediately took a step back.

"Listen hon, do'n be feeling scareda' me. I sees watcha doin'—panning change and all—good stuff! Been watchin' you for awhile. You're good, real good. Makin' 'bout sixty bucks a shift are ya? That's damn fine girl. Buy ya a juice or somethin'?"

Christine shook her head.

"That be fine little girl. That be fine. Do'n want ya should be seen with no nigger eh? I un'nerstand. That cool. Well... be seein' ya around then." The young man headed down the street. Christine felt foolish. She was not refusing his offer because he was black, but because she was nervous around any older man. She didn't mean to hurt his feelings. She hurried after him.

"Wait...just a minute."

The man stopped and waited for Christine to catch up. "I didn't mean to upset you, it's just that I'm new in the city and I don't know too many people. It's not that you're black or anything...I mean, it's not because you're black that I don't want a Coke, it's just...," her voice trailed off. She was embarrassed to discover that she was tongue-tied around the man. He seemed nice enough and he certainly was good looking!

"Okay girl, I un'nerstand when a pretty thing like you wouldn't wanna be seen with no black guy...and like I mean it hurts me...but that's life ain't it?" He turned to walk away again. Christine hurried to keep pace with his long strides.

"No. It's not like that. I think you're great." She wasn't sure why she was responding to him this way, perhaps it was because he seemed so hurt over her refusal. "I'd love to have a drink with you."

He stopped, a smile coming over his face. "Ya sure? Ya not just sayin' that to make me feel good?"

Christine reassured him that she wasn't just being nice and that, in fact, she really liked him. He once again beamed that infectious smile, and taking her by the arm, walked into a nearby restaurant.

"I be Jamus," he said, introducing himself as they slid into a booth. "And you?"

"Christine." She looked down at her lap.

"Howya doin' Christine?" he laughed, taking her hand. "And whatcha be doin' walkin 'round the big streets all by yo'self? A pretty girl like you an' all?"

"Well, I came into the city to spend some time by myself. I wanted to see what it was like. My folks wouldn't let me go, so I sorta left home without telling them. I'm not going back though! Maybe someday, but not now! That is...if I don't run out of money."

The black man seated across from her laughed again. His melodic voice and good humor softened Christine's defenses. "You be listenin' to too much ol' folk talk, little girl. They be from the ancient generation, what with their cars and toasters and such. We be from the now, girl, and we looks after ourselves. You with me girl?" Christine shook her head. He chuckled.

"You been with the ancients too long girl, yo needa be with somma you friends for 'while. I be goin' ta the reggae tonight. Love ta have ya with me, or am I too black for you ta be seen with? Be honest on me now girl, I can tell if you not be truthful."

"No, of course you're not too black for me," Christine grinned in return. "I already told you that. What's this 'reggae' you're talking about?"

"That be the happenin' girl, that be the happenin'! Come on with me, you be havin' some fun!" The sing song cadence of his voice and the gentleness of his manner took her last remaining reservations away. She would go to the *happenin'*, and she would enjoy herself. Maybe Jamus was right. Her parents—correction: *adopted* parents—were from the "ancients," as he put it.

She nodded, "Okay, but you have to stay with me. I won't know anyone, so don't just take me there and leave me. You promise?"

Jamus threw back his head and laughed. "I be goin' ask you the same thing. Don' you be going there, then travlin' off with no other guy. I want you with me, girl, not watchin' you go travlin' away on me." She smiled in return. His accent, although incredibly melodic and almost hypnotic, was difficult to understand. "Travlin?" She had not heard that expression before. "I promise not to go *travlin'*, as you put it. What time does the party start?"

"No party startin' with me not there, so when we go in, that when the party go! What say we eat little girl? I buy for now, then we go do the party thing, okay?" She smiled and nodded.

They ordered a meal and, as they ate, Christine grew even more enchanted by this strange man. The Caribbean language and culture, mixed with American slang and idioms, continued to delight her. She was looking forward to this evening of music and fun with her new friend more than she had anticipated anything in quite some time.

Her tummy full for the first time in a couple days, Christine accepted Jamus' arm as they walked down the street. He stopped beside a metallic gold, luxury sedan. "Here be my car girl, you be driving, okay?"

"Oh, no Jamus, I don't have my license yet!"

"It don't be no bother sweet thing, I know you be the best driver. Here." He handed over a set of keys. Christine was thrilled. She had driven the old truck around the property back home, but never in a fancy car, and certainly not in the city. "Okay, but you have to tell me what to do."

She walked around the car and slipped into the driver's seat. She reached across to open his door, but noted there was no locking knob on the door. "The switch be on the door girl, jus' touch it and all the doors open. It be a magic car!" She laughed and looked for the switch. When she found it, she moved the button to "unlock" so the latch could be lifted from the outside. Jamus opened his door and settled down into the passenger seat. "Okay sweet thing, jus' drive your black angel to da party. I jus' be sittin' here relaxin' and takin' in the scene." She grinned and started the motor.

She eased the expensive automobile into the evening traffic. It was considerably more powerful than the old truck she had driven back home and she had some difficulty maneuvering it for the first few blocks. Once she got the hang of it though, she became more confident, weaving in and out of traffic, revving the motor at stop lights, squealing the tires when the signal turned green. She was having fun for the first time since she had come to the city. Jamus just sat there and laughed, even when she came close to having an accident.

Eventually he gave her directions to the old community hall where the party was being held. They were met by a parking lot jammed with cars. Jamus directed Christine to pull over to the curb and she accidentally bumped into a bus sign bolted to the curb. They both got out of the car and examined the long scratch along the side.

Horrified, she immediately apologized. She expected him to get angry over the damage to his valuable car, but he just shrugged his shoulders. "Hey, little girl, this be part of the scene. This ol' car don' mean nuthin' ta me; it be just the way I move through ma life. If it be scratched, then it still be workin' fine. Don' you be worryin' yourself none, we be gettin' it fixed come the day ahead." Christine was relieved and thanked Jamus profusely for his understanding and for not being angry with her.

He reached out his arms and she snuggled into his embrace. It was so nice to be held and to be with such a kind and gentle man. They turned towards the hall and the sound of music coming from within.

As they entered the building, Christine was swept up by the music, the swaying bodies and the atmosphere. All the men were black, as were many of the women, but immediately she felt at home. Strangers would come up, greet Jamus, then give her a big hug of welcome. She was introduced to dozens of people—each as friendly as the other. No one gave her a bad time or wondered why she was there. She was accepted for who she was: a pretty girl on the arm of a well-respected man!

The party lasted through the night. In the early morning hours, Jamus took her arm and led her to the car. Her head was spinning, partly from the flow of alcohol and marijuana, but also from the party. It was so alive, so exciting! He took the wheel this time, waving goodbye to the group who remained behind.

It was a short drive to a nearby hotel. Christine grew nervous as they drove under the portico and parked the car. "What are we doing here Jamus?" she asked. If he thought that he was going to have sex with her, he had another thought coming! Just because she went to a party with him didn't give him the right to demand payment!

"Jus' relax sweet thing, I don be havin' no lovin' with you. I respect you and that be reason not to push you. I'll jus' be gettin' you a nicer place to lay your little tiredness and be on my way. Or do ya be wantin' ta stay where you been at?" She shook her head.

He led her into the foyer. The lobby was elegantly furnished, far better than she had ever stayed in—even on vacation with her family.

Jamus walked purposefully over to the registration desk. The clerk looked at Christine suspiciously, but after receiving a generous tip from the black man, passed over the card and a pen. It took but a few minutes to complete the necessary paperwork—Jamus paying with cash—and they were on their way up to the assigned room, key in hand. He declined the offer of assistance from a bell hop, but tipped him nonetheless.

The room was bright and airy, with a queen-sized bed, a settee, wing-back chair and the usual industrial grade television, a bureau, writing desk and night stand. The sight of the bed and the thought of enjoying a long sleep after a hot bath, held a lot of appeal for Christine but she would first have to see what Jamus had in mind. She turned to him. "You promised not to make me have sex with you. Does that still hold?"

He laughed. "It sure do, little child, it sure do. I be going back to stay with some brothers, so you be takin' the key here and have yourself a good bed. I be callin' you late in the day now, so just relax an' have yourself one nice sleep. You hear?" She nodded her thanks.

Jamus handed her the key, gave her a quick, almost brotherly peck on the cheek and left. As the door closed behind him, Christine could hardly believe her good fortune. Here she was, just fourteen years old, in the big city and already she had met some really nice people. Jamus was the perfect gentleman. She knew her family would not approve of her going to a party with an older man—particularly a black man—but he hadn't tried anything with her. She wondered where he was staying. He said some "brothers." Maybe he was living with friends. She would have to ask him about that later.

The jangle of the telephone on the bedside table roused Christine from the depths of sleep. She reached for the receiver, noting the time flashing on the clock radio as 4:15 P.M. She'd slept all day! "Hello," she croaked into the receiver. Her voice was raw from all the smoke at the party last night.

"Hello lil' one," greeted Jamus. "It be time you up and goin' girl, don' wan' the day gone and you restin' pretty under no feather blanket. Git yourself up and lookin' good and I be up in a short while to take you out. We got some shoppin' to do, sweet thing, so be ready for greetin' your nigger friend in the soon, okay?" Christine mumbled her understanding and placed the phone back on the table.

She settled back under the covers. To think that yesterday she was panning money from strangers and today she was sleeping in a luxurious bed, had friends, and Jamus was taking her shopping. *Shopping!* She leapt out of bed and headed for the bathroom. She didn't have any clothes other than the ones she wore last night. Her other rags were secured in a coin locker in the bus depot. She remembered that she would have to get them out soon, or she'd lose them. She recalled reading the sticker on the locker door that told her if she left them more than a month they would be removed, probably thrown away.

She dug through the courtesy basket on the bathroom vanity, selecting shampoo, soap, and a combination toothbrush and paste gizmo sealed in crinkly plastic. She brushed her teeth, removing the stale taste of sleep and cigarettes from her mouth. A quick shower and shampoo followed by a brisk rub with the hotel towel and she felt great. She just finished dressing and combing her hair when the knock came to the door. She hurried over.

When the door opened, she threw herself into the arms of Jamus. "Thank you for the room, it was sure great to have a good night's sleep, but boy, am I hungry! It feels like I haven't had anything to eat for days and days." She babbled on, leading Jamus by the hand into the room. He smiled at her. "You sure do look good this day, little girl, sure do look good. I gave the desk some money, so you be staying here long as you feel. Jus' leave that ol' jacket here and we be goin' down and feedin' ourselves some food in the cafe."

The two entered the elevator and dropped to the main floor. The aroma emanating from the kitchen set Christine's taste buds to working overtime. She really was starved! They ordered large portions and sat amicably together in the booth and chatted. When the waitress brought the check, Jamus didn't even glance at it, preferring instead to give Christine a one hundred dollar bill. "You be takin' that as a short loan, okay? You jus' be givin' the girl here the money for the eats, then be puttin' the rest into yo pocket for the future."

Christine took the money and paid for the meal, putting the change into her pocket. "How am I ever going to repay you Jamus?" she asked. "You have done so much for me!"

He just smiled. "We be workin' somethin' out together little girl, not to worry 'bout that now. Let's do some search of the stores and buy you some decent clothes. Don' want no girlfriend of mine lookin' like no trash, do we now?"

Jamus' car was parked in a stall marked "For Handicapped Only." He laughed when he saw Christine look at the restriction. "I be handicapped, I be jus' a poor black boy in the big white city!" He opened her door, then walked around and slid in behind the driver's wheel. He expertly steered the big car out of the hotel parking lot and within a few minutes pulled into a shopping center.

The early evening shoppers were few and far between and the two companions had a riot, darting from store to store, trying on clothes, putting them back, trying on others, and finally making some purchases. Jamus was the picture of pride as he loaded Christine down with slacks, blouses, frilly underwear, coats, shoes, boots and dresses. Jewelry was added to the growing pile, although he did draw the line at an expensive watch she had her eye on. "I can't be gettin' you ever' small thing I would want to. I be glad to buy them for you, but the dent to the door of my car goin' cost me 'bout $500, so I got to watch my money a while." It was the first time he'd made reference to the damage caused by Christine—and she felt guilty. Here he was trying to help her out and she was being greedy!

"I'm sorry Jamus, I guess I just got too excited. I'll help pay for the car and things; I just need some time to get a job."

"Not to worry sweet thing, I be pleased to help you out. You sure is one pretty girl and I be proud to be your boyfriend." It was the second time this day he referred to himself as her boyfriend. It had a nice ring to it. It didn't matter to him if he was older than she, he admired her for what she was. She really liked him and his generosity was almost overwhelming—the hotel, the clothes, the meals—and he didn't want anything in return! It was almost too good to be true.

They returned to the hotel, laden with parcels. Christine took the opportunity to model her new clothes for Jamus. The things were all of excellent quality and her blonde hair and striking appearance accented each piece she put on. They ordered room service, and luxuriated in exotic fare and the lingering excitement of the day's activities.

It was late evening when Jamus explained his problem. The folks he was staying with had put their house up for sale and were moving to another city. This presented a dilemma, as he had nowhere to stay. He explained to Christine that he would have to find an apartment in the next few days, but "could he stay with her until he got things straightened out?" Christine took one look at the new clothes and the luxury of the suite. He promised not to touch her unless she wanted it, and that he would only "stay a few days." She agreed.

The following days flew by in a whirl. She met many of his friends, went to another reggae party, traveled throughout the city, ate at the best restaurants, and made love to Jamus. True to his word, he had not made the first move, but her growing love and dependence on him made the simple act of lovemaking an inevitability. She wanted to remain a part of his life for ever, and undermining her moral code was the fear that he would leave her for someone else if she didn't initiate the sex.

"I be finding my own place tomorrow," he said as they settled down for the evening. "I be needing my own space in awhile. It not be possible for me to live with my friends no more, so I made some calls and be moving out soon." Christine looked over at him. "And what about me? I can't continue here in the hotel; it costs way too much. I don't want to go back living on the street. Can I move in with you?"

"I be wishin' you say that, sweet thing! You sure be right when you tell 'bout this place being too much cash. We can be movin' in together, sort of like man and his wife thing. I be gettin' a job, and you can cook the good meals for me when I come back from workin'." His words struck the right chords in Christine's heart. To be together with Jamus, to share a home—or at least an apartment—to cook his meals and to sleep with him; everything was going to be perfect. "I don't be havin' too much cash right now," he went on. "I had the car by for fixin' and it cost a few. Don't you be worryin' 'bout makin' the dent and all, it be taken care of." He smiled and gave her a hug.

They talked late into the night, dreaming big dreams, making great plans, and enjoying the warmth and closeness of their love. At least that is what it all appeared to be. Things, however, have a way of changing.

• • •

Unknown to Christine, her parents had mounted an intensive search. They had officially registered her as a missing person and had hired a private detective to follow all leads. Additionally, various police forces were alerted, and a number of agencies for missing children notified.

Both Cam and Alana loved this bright little girl too much to wash their hands of her and forget about her. They knew that she was having difficulty adjusting to the knowledge of her adoption and, the longer she was away from home and family, the greater the risk to her wellbeing.

• • •

During the following six months, Christine and Jamus moved into a nice apartment, and things went along smoothly, until one day there was a scowl on his face. "I don' be knowin' how to tell you this sweet babe, but I ain' got no money left. What with the car, the apartment, you, my own costs, not much left to go on about. We gotta do ourselves some hard thinkin' here."

Christine sat beside him. "I'll do anything for you Jamus. I love you. I don't want us to break up just because we don't have enough money. Is there anything I can do to help?"

Jamus looked, first at her, then at the floor, in a display of embarrassment. "Well sweet child, there be one thing, and I wan' you to know I is ashamed to even bring it up, but we in big trouble right now." He paused until she pressed him further.

"I don' want you should be ashamed of your nigger. I don' talk 'bout myself that much, I much afraid you be leavin' me for some other brother and I can' take that should it be happenin'. You don' know me real well, an' you sure don' know what I used to do. If I tell you now, I worry you be leavin' me and not comin' back. Un'nerstand?" Christine threw her arms around him.

"Oh, Jamus. There is nothing you can say that would make me leave you, nothing! I don't care if you're a bank robber or a drug dealer. I promise that whatever you tell me about your past I will still love you and stay with you."

He looked her in the eye. "You just be sayin' that 'cause you don' know me girl. If I told you I was doing the drugs, you'd up and leave me like that." He snapped his fingers.

She professed her love for him more strongly and promised that she would never leave him. "After all, it's because of me you're in this fix. I was the one that scratched your car. I was the one you rented the hotel for. And, you bought me all those clothes. I can't leave you even if I wanted to—I owe you too much!" This was the opening he'd been waiting for.

"Well, sweet thing, I gotta' take the chance. I be tellin' you. For the long time up 'till I be meetin' you, I had some girls who worked for me. They would have sex with a guy and I be makin' sure they okay and things, and we split the cash 50–50. We be makin' 'bout ten grand a week and livin' high. Then you come into this nigger's heart, and BAM! I fall in love and don' be workin' the girls no more. Then I pay the car and things and now don' have no money." He hung his head and would not look at her.

Christine snuggled against him. "I told you…it doesn't matter. I don't care if you had other girls and if they worked for you selling sex. You gave it up for me! That tells me how much you love me! To be willing to give up ten thousand dollars a week, just for me, is the biggest compliment I ever got. No one ever cared for me like that!" She put her arms around him. "Maybe you can do that again? I won't mind. I know I caused you to do this, so if you do it again, I won't mind."

He shook his head. "Them girls, I just let them go to another man. He be workin' them now for him. Ain' no way I could work 'em any more, they be gone now. I guess you just gon' have to live in the car with this here nigger 'til we get some money somehow. Jus' ain' no way to do it no more. Things be changed with you and all." He looked at her. "You know what I mean sweet thing?"

The girl nodded. "Yes I do…but, and I don't like saying this, but am I as pretty as those other girls? Would I be able to work for you? That is, if you would want me to. I wouldn't want to do anything you didn't want me to do."

"Oh, sweet child. You sure be good lookin'. Much better lookin' than them girls. I don' want you havin' sex with no strangers, but I don' see what else we be able to do. Maybe we do it just a few times to get some cash together. Maybe even get some of them girls back and you and me can run 'em together. What you think girl?"

She nodded enthusiastically. She wanted to know all about the other girls. Where they worked, what they did, how they did it. She'd seen prostitutes, but had never met any. She hung on his every word. When he started describing how she would work, he made it seem glamorous and exciting. When he added in the dream of how they would eventually have twenty girls working for them, with her as the manager while he looked after any other problems, Christine positively glowed with anticipation.

They discussed the "business" late into the night, snuggled tightly together once again. Christine felt so safe, so secure, eyes closed and lying in his arms. Jamus on the other hand, lay there smiling. It had taken time, taken money, but she was ready.

The following evening, he instructed her on what to wear, how to walk, how to give "the look" and how to check if the customer was an undercover cop. She was nervous, yet excited, embarking on her new "career" as she saw it. He took Christine down to the stroll and, after introducing her to several girls who were working, asked them to pass on the message to their "men." Then he left her there under the tutelage of an older, more experienced pro.

She turned her first trick within a half hour of being out there. The regular parade of johns were quick to spot new flesh and quickly honed in on her. The constant strain of the street was tiring, but by the end of her shift she had collected four hundred and thirty dollars. When Jamus came by to pick her up, she handed over the entire roll to him. He peeled off a hundred, returning the remainder to her. "You should take half. That was our deal!" Christine pleaded.

"Oh no, girl, maybe later we go that, but this night you be earning' every bit. If I wasn't broke like I is, you be takin' it all. I jus' need some to get me things for now. You be good girl! You be one good worker! I proud of you!" She fairly glowed in his praises.

If the day had not been as long or as tiring, or if either of them had been as alert as they should have, they would have not have missed spotting the tan minivan following a discrete distance behind.

Jamus, for all his street smarts, had the one fundamental flaw common in all pimps: arrogance. He had been so successful for so long, he believed his own reputation. He believed himself to be "undo-able." He was "live," a "super fly," a "mack daddy," a man with a reputation and respect. What he neglected to consider was that there was another side to the street, one walked by people who were determined to cut his career as short as possible.

Long before Christine had entered the picture, they'd been watching him. Files were made, photos taken, wiretaps run, surveillance conducted, and informants consulted. They were the vice cops whose sole reason for existence was to jail predators like Jamus. It took a long time to build the case, but the emergence of the new girl, and the information from her parents as to her actual age, had placed the last piece of evidence in their laps.

Nightly, they watched as Christine would be dropped off by Jamus, conduct her business, then meet and turn over the money to him when she was finished. Each transaction was noted—many photographed.

The actual arrest was anticlimactic. After so many months of hard work, it was over quickly. Jamus was taken into custody and placed in a holding cell while the paper work was processed. Christine was taken to an interview room where she met her parents for the first time in over a year. The tension surrounding the circumstances of Jamus's arrest, the isolation from her parents Christine had initiated—compounded by the embarrassment of being caught working as a prostitute—made the meeting awkward for all of them.

Identities were established, statements taken and Christine was free to go home with her parents. She was disoriented and confused by the speed of what had transpired. The vice cop had told her that, in addition to Christine, Jamus was running three other girls. He'd never stopped his pimping activity, even though he had told Christine she was the only one. She felt betrayed and angry and, when given the opportunity, signed a statement confirming Jamus's involvement in prostitution. He was subsequently charged with *Procuring A Minor*, *Living On The Avails of Prostitution*, and *Directing and Controlling a Prostitute*. He faced a total of 45 years in a federal prison. Only the presentation of evidence stood in the way.

• • •

For the next eighteen months, while the case worked its way through the courts, it was frequently adjourned by lawyers for one reason or another, Christine remained with her parents.

The application for bail by Jamus was denied and he remained behind bars. A preliminary hearing was held and the testimony of the police and witness were presented. A trial date was set.

Because there was considerable evidence, six days had been set aside in the court calendar for the trial. The first portion of the prosecution's case came when the evidence from the police was brought forward. They presented their observations and surveillance data. They had graphs and charts that detailed Jamus's movements throughout the thirteen months he'd been under investigation. Hotel receipts were produced showing how he had paid for rooms for the various prostitutes under his influence. Utility bills were entered as evidence he had maintained several apartments at the same time. Recordings of telephone conversations were played for the court that chronicled his many business transactions with other pimps and customers. It was a flawlessly detailed presentation of the prosecution's case. The final part of the case was Christine's testimony.

• • •

"Do you swear to tell the truth, the whole truth, and nothing but the truth, so help you God?" The formality of the courtroom and the demeanor of the court clerk, as she read the words to Christine, were almost overwhelming. Seeing her former lover in the accused's chair brought all the memories flooding back. Memories of exciting rides in his big car, shopping sprees where she spent thousands of dollars on clothing, parties, and meals in fancy restaurants.

As Jamus looked at her and smiled sweetly, those memories blocked out the pain of lonely nights, of strangers using her body, and her feelings of disgust. All she could see was the mesmerizing gaze as he held her in his focus. Like that first meeting on the street, she felt herself fall under his spell once again.

In spite of the valiant effort by the prosecution, Christine refused to implicate Jamus in any act for which he was charged. The evidence put forward by the detectives was solid and implicated the accused in a number of crimes, but without the direct testimony of the victim, the judge had no option but to dismiss the charges and release him from custody.

Within days of his release, Jamus was back in business. Christine, after her refusal to testify against him, never returned home.

• • •

Leaving the court house, she abandoned her distraught parents standing on the steps, walked down the sidewalk and back into the life of prostitution. The memories generated by the sight of Jamus had such a hold over her, that the eighteen months she had been separated from her pimp were dismissed without a backward glance.

Christine became one of Jamus' regular street prostitutes. In punishment for signing on him, he placed a one thousand dollar "street fee" on her. In addition, he raised her daily quota to eight hundred dollars. She mildly objected, but his explanation made some sort of twisted sense to Christine and she redoubled her efforts to attain her previous relationship with him.

"You be causing' me some serious grief little girl," he had explained on the first night they were together. "I been in the man's jail for over the year now and my money be all gone. With the lawyers and such, I be broke sweet child, so you be have to work real hard." He went on to lay out his expectations for her working income, as well as the thousand dollars which was her "share" of his legal expenses.

Over the following weeks, Christine, and the three other girls working for Jamus, produced almost four thousand dollars a day. They worked seven days a week, and by the end of the month had turned over to Jamus the incredible sum of $104,000.00. His control was total.

In spite of her best efforts, Christine could not bring in her required quota every single day. There were times when the stroll was "soft" and the customers picky. On those occasions, Jamus would become enraged, accusing the girls, and particularly Christine, of being "lazy ho's," of being disrespectful and disloyal. He would beat them, careful never to mark their faces—the assets upon which he was building his fortune. But as his outrage grew, so did his violence, and inevitably, he used his fists on Christine's face. With a blackened eye, cut lip, and swollen nose, she was sent back to the street with a two hundred dollar increase in her quota. To make a thousand dollars in a night, looking the way she did, would be almost impossible.

Her second trick made the offer she'd always turned away: a condomless lay. For an extra one hundred dollars, the customer wanted to have intercourse with Christine free from the confines of a latex condom. Realizing that this was her only chance to make her quota and avoid a scene with Jamus, she reluctantly agreed. She was well versed in the dangers associated with unprotected sex. She had been schooled, both by Jamus and by the agency that came by nightly in a van to hand out condoms and give medical advice. She knew all this, but the pressure to produce her quota overcame her normal caution. "Maybe this once is okay. Maybe if I make my quota he'll let me rest awhile. Maybe...maybe...maybe."

Two months passed and Jamus still did not reduce her quota. The nights were long and dangerous as she strove to bring back to her man the amount of money he demanded. Christine resorted to tactics she had never previously employed—picking the pockets of her customers, selling crack cocaine to other prostitutes, shoplifting, and pawning the stolen merchandise—anything to make a thousand dollars a day. Her health failed markedly and, when a patrolling vice officer—one of the same detectives who had testified against Jamus during that ill-fated trial—found her lying in an alley, she was finally taken to a medical clinic.

A full battery of tests were conducted. In addition to malnutrition, and a serious condition brought on through poor feminine hygiene, she had contracted several sexually transmitted diseases. A full blood workup was conducted, additional tests taken, and she was advised to return in a week for the results.

The day the tests results were due, Christine returned to the stroll. She'd decided not to contact the Health Clinic—she didn't have money for prescriptions anyway, so what was the point? The evening began and she had turned three tricks before midnight. It looked like a busy night and she'd reach her quota without resorting to roll jobs. The social services van rounded the corner and pulled up beside her. Because she needed a coffee and some condoms, she slid back the side door and hopped inside.

Seated at the rear of the van was one of the public health nurses and the same detective who had taken her into the clinic suffering from exhaustion and malnutrition the week before.

"What's all this about?" she asked, mildly alarmed, directing her question to the two. "Why are you guys here?"

It was the detective who replied. "You have to come in with us Christine. You can't work out here anymore."

"Why not? What's happened?"

This time it was the nurse's turn to speak. "Christine, the results of your tests have come back. I was hoping you would come into the clinic but since you didn't...I decided to come out with the van. I asked the detective to come with me."

"How come? I mean you just took some tests and stuff, how come I can't work anymore? I've been keeping out of trouble. I don't give you guys a hard time do I?" Christine directed her protests to the detective.

"No Christine, you don't give us a hard time, but you do have to come in to the clinic. The nurse here just asked me to go along in case there was any problems. Since there isn't, why don't we just drive down to the clinic now and she can explain all the medical stuff to you there? Okay?"

By this time, Christine's nervousness had turned to fear. She looked from one to the other. "I'm getting out of here right now!" She started to slide back the door. The detective moved forward and blocked her exit. "No Christine, I told you that you can't work anymore, and I mean it. Now close the door so we can go to the clinic. We don't want to scare you, but this is serious."

Christine started to cry. Fear had been replaced by terror. Never had she seen such sorrow on the faces of relative strangers. With her heart beating wildly, she nodded her consent. The van—with Christine, the nurse, the detective—moved eight blocks to the rear of the clinic.

The discussion that took place, late that night, was technical and academic, but it confirmed the deepest fears of the little girl who had run away from her parents' home in the country just a few short years ago. Christine's tests had returned HIV Positive. The duty nurse introduced

Christine to a doctor who outlined what lay ahead. Although they tried all they could to provide her with information and advice, she rejected their assistance.

In spite of the cautions from the doctor and the admonitions of the vice detective, Christine returned to the street. Jamus threw her out as soon as she told him the results of her test.

She is working to keep herself alive just one more day. Although full-blown AIDS has not yet arrived, it is inevitable.

• • •

Christine is now eighteen years old and all alone. She is just waiting to die.

7

Players in the Game

Those who have been there can't explain.
Those who haven't, can't understand.

IF you consider Tanya, Kara, Jackie, Sukan, and Christine—and all
other child prostitutes—as victims, you're correct! If you feel
compelled to address the reasons they became involved, and you want
to take a stand: to help, to prevent, to rescue, to restore—that is
understandable. However, we need to act from a knowledge base, from a
point of strength—not solely from a sense of righteousness or outrage. To
build our understanding, we need to know about the "players", and to
illuminate the "game" itself.

There are two major players—the pimp, and the prostitute.

This chapter begins with an examination of the pyschopathology of a
pimp. By understanding his personality, his need for power and wealth,
his quest for rank in the hierarchy of pimps, his pathological lies, and his
criminal versatility, we can profile the enemy.

Only then can we begin to understand the cycle of deceit, coercion,
threats, and violence that this smooth-talking predator perpetrates on his
victims.

In the previous chapters, we've been exposed to some typical stories of
the girls and their relationships with the ones who control them. We now
have a sense of how the pimp operates. He's glib. He has a superficial
charm, and the ability to manipulate and use people. He's violent. We
can, however, provide a more detailed description of the psycho-social
makeup of a pimp.

We can't deny that pimps are effective at what they do—they attract,
recruit and enslave young girls. How do they do that? It's not necessarily
their looks, for many pimps do not fall into society's common definition
of handsome. It isn't money. Many of them, in spite of "flash rolls" and
expensive habits are penniless without their girls' income. Most are on
the verge of poverty, owning nothing more than the clothes on their backs

and an impressive car. Not particularly known for being articulate, many pimps have difficulty in expressing words properly.

If it isn't their looks, their money, or their language—what makes them so effective? What do they have that would cause a young woman to abandon everything she believed in, subject herself to beatings, rapes, and ridicule, and enslave herself to another human being? Let me explain it, using a quote from a certain "live" pimp who, when being examined by a prosecutor—while giving testimony in his own defense—made the comment, "There ain't no rules, that's why I win."

If we accept that premise, then everything else starts to fall into place.

As members of a civilized society, we play by certain rules: the rules of common decency, of conscience, of a sense of concern for our fellow human beings. We also have to play by the law—the same law that guarantees even a pimp the right to legal counsel, the right to litigate if he feels subjected to an unreasonable search, the right to bail, and the right to a speedy trial. Protected by the law, and unhampered by any rules, the pimp freely designs the game so that he alone retains control. Just when we get a handle on him, he not only changes the rules, he moves or replaces the entire game board.

Our rules are different from his. Where we do not use violence to influence another person's decisions, the pimp regularly employs that technique. We do not lie, whereas he cannot exist without deceit. We work for our income, but this predator lives by exploiting others.

He becomes much easier to understand and to deal with if we accept one basic premise: the pimp, in order to conduct his business in the manner he does, is a psychopath.

Psychopathology of the Pimp

The "straight" world is generally unfamiliar with the operation of a street predator. We often have difficulty in coming to grips with the idea of one person existing solely to prey on the physical and emotional weakness of another. If we substituted the word *pimp* by another descriptive noun, such as *dictator, cult leader, tyrant,* or *despot,* this type of individual becomes more recognizable. In fact, all those descriptions fit the pimp.

Personality

The character of a person—who engages in the type of devastating exploitation employed by pimps—forms early in life. Most pimps had a childhood characterized by a domineering, unloving father who demanded unquestioning obedience from the youngster, and themselves treated women as objects to be used and controlled. We know that pimping activities are often trans-generational. In some families, grandfathers, fathers, and sons have all engaged in the procuring of women for sexual abuse and misuse.

Certainly we can't stop there in our analysis. Many men have had tough upbringings, yet have had the courage and the will to rise above it and become outstanding contributors to society. History is replete with stories of great men coming from disadvantaged and abusive backgrounds. There are more characteristics in the psychopathology of the pimp than just an abusive father.

Early in childhood, the budding pimp displays behavioral problems, often from his grade school years. He exhibits controlling tactics over peers and uses a combination of guile and violence to attain his goals.

Juvenile delinquency becomes part of his repertoire as he grows into his teen years and, at this time, he begins to demonstrate his warped attitude toward women. He learns that he can dominate some girls and women through the force of his personality. He becomes promiscuous in dating practices, yet seeks to hold onto girls whom he has dated in the past, viewing them as his property. He will often go to great lengths—up to and including murder—to retain that control.

He learns to live a parasitic lifestyle, surviving on the goods, money, and services provided by others. He hones his skills as a master manipulator, using a combination of guilt and fear to attain and retain control over others. Not a planner, he has great difficulty conceptualizing the future, preferring to live for the moment.

In his late teen years, he only needs a reason to propel him into the next phase—the procuring of young women. As he moves deeper into the world of clubs, bars, alcohol and drugs, that motivation soon becomes apparent. He finds that he has a need for money and personal status. That desire, coupled with his ability to use the people around him, form a deadly combination. Over the months and years, he forms a personality that has become synonymous with the word "pimp."

The Hierarchical Structure

The predatory pimp structures his surroundings so that he is the "chief executive officer" of his own organization. Initially, he performs all major tasks himself. These include recruiting, training, directing, controlling, marketing, security, finances, discipline, and social outings. Eventually, he will delegate and coerce other workers to fill some of these roles as he builds his business. As CEO, his power is absolute, unrelenting, and ruthless.

He learns that in straight society, those who attain positions of power and influence have titles bestowed on them. Titles such as *chief, judge,* and *mayor* impress him because they reflect high status or position. Many others are honorary: *Your Honor, Reverend* or even *Sir.* Recognizing that he will never attain these titles through legitimate means, he adopts trendy or theatrical "street names" in an effort to enhance his standing in "the life." Names such as *Dragon, Dance, Sweet* or *Diamond* are just a few he typically selects for himself. Other names such as *Que, Trey, T.J.* or *Taz* are diminutives of their real names, but nonetheless serve to identify them as serious players in the game. His ideal focuses on being regarded as the "baddest" player, the one with the most respect. He doesn't take kindly to second spot.

Desire for Power and Wealth

As one pimp explained, "This is the game! The challenge is to be the best, to gather more girls, more money, more influence, more respect than the other players. If one pimp has four girls well, you got to take some of his away, or get more yourself. It's better if you bump some of his—that increases your respect and power. They gotta be good ho's too, so they can bring in the money!"

The pimp may sacrifice everything as he progresses deeper into the game. In the early years, he often forms an attachment to some of his girls, favoring one over the other, buying them special gifts, and even splitting the money they make. As the years pass, the addiction of the life draws the worst of his character from deep within. He loses any sense of kindness, interpreting it as "softness" in a game of hard ball. In order to retain his status, he becomes more abusive and more violent. He takes risks he never would have dared to take in his early years.

In most criminal activities, the perpetrator becomes more cautious, more calculating, as time passes. Curiously, in his bid to stay on top, the pimp takes reckless chances that ultimately lead to his downfall. Where he once would have used charm and persuasion to initiate a girl into the life, he now uses force. If he does not, and loses a girl to a budding pimp or, worse yet, she testifies against him, other players view him as "dead"—out of the game, a subject of ridicule, of no account.

Pathological Liar

Very early in life, the future pimp learns that he can attain his goals by devious means. School, sports, social connections, even his love affairs, all have an element of untruth to them. He embellishes his abilities as a sports star, although in truth most are not athletic. He exaggerates the connections he has in the underworld of crime, even though criminals consider pimps the lowest rung on their hierarchical ladder—lower even than a pedophile because often a pimp supplies the pedophile with the focus of his perversion.

The pimp spends an excessive amount of time perpetuating the myth that he is an exceptional lover. He becomes enraged when women who have slept with him debunk that illusion.

Over the years, the pimp develops an inability to be truthful. He's learned to deceive and manipulate and, even if the truth would help him, goes out of his way to fabricate lies. He has been successful in conning young impressionable girls, and attempts, often with some degree of success, to carry those techniques over into mainstream society. Many police officers experience the frustration of hearing a pimp take the stand at a trial, and spin a tale for the judge that would, as often as not, be accepted.

I recall one particular case where five young girls charged their pimp. Additionally, he faced criminal indictments involving weapons and stolen property in which the police, not the children, were the witnesses. At the conclusion of the trial, the judge threw out every charge, preferring to believe the unsupported testimony of the pimp rather than the well investigated, documented, and corroborated evidence of eleven separate witnesses.

Lack of Friends

The pimp is usually single and always unfaithful. Incapable of sustaining any type of permanent relationship, he does not preserve any friendships of his own. At best, he maintains a few acquaintances. His need to manipulate and control drives those around him to the outer edge of the criminal fraternity.

Impulsive, with no realistic life plans, the pimp entertains grandiose ideas: one minute he dreams of owning a restaurant or bar, the next of operating a travel bureau, and the next he fantasizes being a stockbroker. A big talker, his schemes seldom come to fruition. Often, he will gather some acquaintances, sketch a fanciful plan, collect a few thousand dollars to develop the dream, then allow the entire process to fall down around them.

Ingenuous and erratic, he's not known for punctuality nor for his reliability in paying his debts. According to lawyers, the pimp is always an undesirable client. They admit, in confidence, that they would rather defend a murderer than a pimp.

Criminal Versatility

Over the years, I have had active pimps openly come to my office and introduce themselves, offering to explain the various "misunderstandings" that had taken place between themselves and girls they had supposedly spurned and were now, they typically claim, "out for revenge!" Usually they embark on their version of reality, using half-truths or preposterous illustrations that the listener cannot verify. Their stories, often complex and detailed, contain more fantasy than fact.

One pimp claimed that he was a consultant to a women's gymnastic program and that some of the clients, envious of his popularity, sparked allegations of prostitution. Upon investigation, the detective learned the pimp frequented the gym. True, he often helped women with weights or aerobics; and yes, many were envious of his contact with the women. On the surface, it appeared that the pimp could be right, but stories like his often weave fact and fiction in an intricate web.

Further investigation revealed that he paid for his membership in the gym—he'd never been even the most casual of employees. He was using the facility as a center for recruiting but he also shrewdly contrived a story that would be defensible in court. A very knowledgeable and dedicated detective can sort through the illusions and lies to arrive at the truth of the matter. The officer then faces the task of debunking the alibi. He must then convince a judge that the pimp, far from being an altruistic individual with social concerns, is a predator seeking to recruit unsuspecting young women into an incredibly destructive lifestyle.

Recruiting: Deceit and The Beginning of Destruction

What person in their right mind would involve themselves with a pimp if they were honestly knowledgeable about his actions? How could they succumb to his tactics? If a pimp was *honest* in his recruiting, his "rap" might sound like this:

Hello there. My name is Kevin, but I go by the street name Snake. I earn my living as a pimp. If you are not familiar with how we work, I'd like a few minutes of your time to explain. First I will seduce you with promises and dreams that I have no intention of fulfilling. In order to make you believe my promises, I'll buy you a few cheap trinkets, some flashy clothes, and give you a ride in my car. After you have fallen in love with me, I will pass you on to several strangers who will rape you, and in return will give me some money.

As we progress in our relationship, I'll do everything I can to cut you off from all your former friends and family, as I force you to become totally dependent on me. I will do your thinking for you: tell you when to get up, when to eat, and what to wear. You will no longer make any decisions on your own. You will work as a prostitute for fifteen hours a day and will turn over every cent you make to me. If you try to retain even part of your earnings, I'll beat you with my fists and feet, or whip you with a coat hanger until you bleed.

I will not allow you to go to the hospital when you are sick or injured, nor will I allow you to have friends other than the ones I pick for you. On occasion I'll give you some drugs or alcohol, but you must still produce an average of $500 a day by having sex with strangers. You'll turn the all money over to me. If you become diseased or in any fashion unable to work, I'll sell you to someone else for as much money as I can get out of them. If you go to the police, or in any way attempt to leave me, I will intimidate you, threaten you or your family. Maybe I'll even try to have you killed.

"Now...when can you start work?"

No one, knowing all these details, would volunteer to become a part of something so debasing, so destructive. In order for the pimp to continue in his lifestyle, he must constantly employ devious strategies in his recruiting manner.

Illusions of Special Status

The pimp views himself as both different and special from mainstream society. His pattern of thought diverges from the norm. Whereas the vast majority of people in our culture share similar values, particularly when it comes to children, the pimp stands out as a deviant. The pimp, like the child molester, regards children as pawns to use in whatever fashion he chooses. Even hard core criminals hold child molesters and pimps in contempt. Within the penal system, when a child rapist enters a prison, officials must make special provisions to protect him against aggression from the other prisoners.

Self-centered and narcissistic, many pimps spend hours each day working out in a gym, building their bodies. Some claim to have a black belt in karate or in one of the other martial arts, although on investigation, I have never found one who had actually attained that level of skill. They may buy clothes to reflect their supposed special status or drive cars that are flamboyant and colorful, but few have more than these superficial images of wealth.

In order to keep his self-defined special status, the pimp behaves as if he was the only one in his circle who judges what is important. Although incredibly influenced by those who have respect in the game, he adopts an attitude of omniscience, and he believes that he alone decides the flow of events. To foster that illusion, he effectively uses his ability to deceive and manipulate as he exerts control over his "family."

One pimp, in explaining his particular technique, illustrated his idea of control by boasting that if he kept a girl away from her family for two days, she was his. During these two days, he would repeat, over and over, how her parents were domineering, did not understand her, and did not care about her. He then would give her a chance to phone them. Knowing the typical reaction of overwrought parents as well as he does, he simply sat back as the confrontation ensued and the parents confirmed his analysis.

Typically, the young girl's parents expressed anger, intolerance and resentment, and would demand that she return home. If she attempted to explain herself, they would cut her off and tell her not to return until she's ready to obey the family rules. She would be crying when she got off the phone and who would be there to comfort her? Why, the pimp of course! He could solve all problems, provide all comfort, and control all circumstances. She was his.

Social Acceptance of the Pimp

Hard as it may be to accept, mainstream society often becomes the pimp's greatest asset in securing new girls. Movies, and popular culture portray him as a mysterious fellow, with an almost hypnotic effect on women. Depicted as the man to whom distressed women run, the pimp's mythological role becomes one of the universal caretaker, protecting them from themselves and social injustice.

Our culture portrays the prostitute as a woman with a heart of gold, a bright, individualistic person treated badly by the world, who has rebelled, and chosen a life that eventually will make all her dreams come true. Hollywood fosters this image through films such as the one in which a wealthy man in an exotic sports car "rescues" a glamorous street walker and whisks her away to a life of riches, travel, and romance. Her devastating past life dissolves into a "pretty" new world.

Courts reflect this attitude as well. Many judges are under the belief that young girls seek out dangerous liaisons in order to embark on a life of prostitution. Officers of the court compound this error by mistakenly believing that the pimp has some significant—or even sympathetic—role to play in a prostitute's life. They perceive the pimp stationed close to the working girl to ensure her safety, making sure that a customer doesn't rough her up, and protecting her from police harassment.

Unfortunately, social workers, health care practitioners, church leaders, and educators—the very people who should be helping these children—share this view. I've spoken to dozens who perceive the girls as sexually promiscuous children, who have consciously embarked on a lifestyle of her own choosing! This viewpoint, unfortunately, is not exclusive to these professions; too often, we find it echoed by the majority of people in our culture.

Politicians and police forces reluctantly turn a blind eye to pimps and prostitutes when other issues, apparently more critical, plague their cities or strain their budgets. How often have we heard these pathetic observations: prostitution is a "victimless crime," or the solution to the "prostitution problem" lies in annexing the sex industry in "red light districts," or that society should legalize, regulate, and tax the trade?

With archaic attitudes such as these, is it any wonder the pimp has such easy pickings? Our society calls prostitution a victimless crime—but is it?

The Prostitute: The Real Victim

As a society, we must fully comprehend that adults have victimized many of these children from the time they were toddlers. Frequently, through physical, emotional, or sexual abuse they are casualties of their own families. They run away and are further victimized on the streets, by the pimps, and by society itself. Researchers tell us that the average age of females entering prostitution in North America is thirteen and a half years old. Statistics tell us that most prostitutes, about 85%, come from abusive backgrounds, although, in recent years about 15% of the girls arriving on the streets are from good, solid homes. Smooth-talking predators who move—almost with impunity—through our communities, seduce these children into the life.

What does being a prostitute do the minds and bodies of these little girls? Until we understand what happens to these children—mentally and physically—we have difficulty shedding our preconceptions of prostitutes and prostitution, and shifting our perceptions of them from children who have made bad choices to children who have suffered the most degrading victimization our culture can endure.

Physical Damage

Picture, for just a moment, a young girl in her early teens. She styles her long hair swept back from her forehead like all her chums; she wears baggy jeans and an old plaid shirt. It's the uniform of the day, worn by all her crowd. With her face scrubbed and shiny, she heads for her eighth grade Social Studies class. She makes her way down the crowded hallway of the junior high, chatting with her friends about rock groups, boys, the teachers, shopping, and where she's going this coming weekend. At the age of experiencing new-found independence, expressing rebellion, and focusing on self-esteem issues, she spends most of her time with peers. Fairly typical, this youngster is just being what she should be: a young girl.

Now, picture her a year later. She's just been rescued from a trick pad where a pimp forced her to work as a prostitute. Investigators determine that this child averaged eighteen acts of sexual intercourse daily—the highest number was forty-two men in one night. She has not eaten properly for months; she's foraged on whatever she could from fast food outlets or convenience stores, existing mostly on diet sodas and candy bars. Many times she went hungry for days on end. She has not had a medical checkup nor has she seen a dentist or optometrist for months.

Angry red welts, evidence of repeated beatings, scar her back and buttocks. With two teeth knocked loose, and an open sore on her right shin where someone kicked her with heavy work boots, she requires immediate medical attention. Prior to falling in with a pimp she weighed a healthy 110 pounds but in the intervening year she's lost weight and now tips the scales at just under 88 pounds. Malnourished, her hair has thinned and is falling out, her eyes are sunken and dull, and she suffers from rickets. A medical examination reveals she's infested with body lice, and further tests reveal she also has gonorrhea.

One of only a handful of child prostitution recovery centers in North America, all operated privately, will admit her. Her convalescence will continue for almost two years before she physically recovers from the damage suffered in the trick pad.

Emotional Damage

During the past twelve months, this little girl has missed nine family holidays, including two Christmases. Her older sister gave birth to a baby ten months ago and she has yet to see him. Grandma died last spring, and because she didn't know about the death, she missed the chance to say one last goodbye. In addition to self-imposed guilt, she feels an incredible sense of loss. She has spent almost ten percent of her life apart from her family.

She deeply regrets her time as a prostitute, and feels deep shame as she recalls the details of what she went through and the acts in which she participated. She remains cynical and suspicious of the straight world because she has seen many so-called upstanding citizens use her for their own selfish pleasures. Repeatedly, her pimp and other street people cautioned her not to trust anyone: the police, social workers, or her parents.

Now, of course, she knows she must trust them, but her faith in the system has become alienated by the counter-message so deeply ingrained in her.

The isolation and trauma she's experienced forced her to make new friends, all of whom remain trapped in the game. She worries about the two girls in the trick pad—friends with whom she laughed and cried, who supported her—they're still there, continuing life without her. In the quiet of the night, her memories flood back, and she knows that unless something radical happens, the chances of her ever seeing her street friends again are remote. Her emotions, however, remain suppressed in the desolation of loneliness.

Cognitive Difficulties

Before heading to the recovery center, we take her for a quick meal. In the restaurant, we get the first hint that she has difficulty in structuring thought patterns. Faced with the awesome task of having to choose from among four types of salad dressing, she panics. Which one to choose? Should it be the French? Maybe the Thousand Island? What about the Italian? Or should she pick the Blue Cheese?

She picks first one, then another. She lifts a bottle, begins to pour it, then she quickly sets it down and looks in my direction to see if I approve. Finally, after sitting quietly for several minutes, she asks my advice. "Which one should I take?" We eliminate them slowly, one at a time, until she makes a selection. This is only the first of many challenges to come. For a year now, her pimp hasn't allowed her to make any decisions—in what to wear, what to eat, where to go or what to do. Her pimp dictated every aspect of her life, controlled every choice, and made all her decisions. Ironically, she went to the street for freedom, and found, instead, the ultimate in subjugation.

Her memory is not what it once was. She cannot recall simple geography, political parties, or her parents anniversary. The passage of time means little to her. Researchers tell us that the mind, composed of short-term, mid-term, and long-term memory, reacts to any lasting trauma by wiping away much of the memory and replacing it by the details of the trauma itself. Drug use and poor nutrition have further affected her memory. For now she has repressed all thoughts of the past; she appears disoriented, numbed to her environment. A mechanism of self-protection, the numbness shields her from reality: from her memories; from making moment-to-moment decisions; from the horror she has endured for months.

Over the next three to five years, memories will return as she awakens in the dark of night, her body bathed in sweat and her heart pounding. The nightmares she will experience will be terrifying, ripping her from sleep and forcing her to relive those frightful days of the past. The vividness of the dreams will gradually fade, but will never leave her completely. She must deal with her past as best she can.

Legal Difficulties

Working as a prostitute has destroyed her personal identity. She needs new identification cards: a birth certificate, health credentials, social insurance documents—even a library card. In an effort to help her, the officer searches for her proper name, her aliases, and date of birth in the police computer. The resulting printout reveals more trouble.

She has a number of outstanding warrants. Picked up several times for shoplifting, she never appeared in court. She had received several local bylaw infractions that netted a few hundred dollars in assessments. Using fake I.D., she rented an apartment for her pimp. There was considerable damage done to the suite, and the landlord has demanded restitution. He wants his money.

In one of her earlier court appearances, the judge gave her a period of probation as well as community service hours, but she has never met with her probation officer, nor even attempted to complete the assigned work. She now faces several trials, owes money to the court system, has to work off her community commitments, and must testify at upcoming hearings against her pimp.

Her legal difficulties have just begun.

The young girl is pregnant. The stage has long since passed for her to consider abortion as a viable option. For the first several months she never even realized that she was carrying a child, alerting to the fact only when her tummy became fuller and her friends noticed her growing size. She does not know who the father is—it could be one of a hundred possibilities. She does not even know whether the baby will be white, black, Asian or Hispanic.

What is her legal status and the status of her soon to be born child? Will she, at fifteen, keep the baby? Taking into consideration the emotional damage she has already undergone, will Children's Aid seek a court order to seize the child, or will her parents elect to raise the baby for her? What happens if, a year or two from now, a man comes forward and lays claim to the child—will there be another court battle?

Social Difficulties

Losing one year of schooling does not in itself present a major problem, but combined with her upcoming therapy and counseling, she will encounter significant difficulties in the years ahead. Her loss of cognitive ability, coupled with other psychological and sociological problems, will present almost insurmountable obstacles.

How can this child, who has lived in the violent world of drugs, gangs, prostitution, and robbery, ever hope to reconnect with her peers? Her former school friends have all rejected her and moved on with their lives. They know she's off the street, but they don't phone or visit. How can she compare the experience of going on a date to a bowling alley with a sixteen year old boy, when she has lived in a world of fast cars, drugs, nightclubs, and all night binges?

Her family tries not to let her revelations shock them and they struggle to adjust their shattered lives. Gone are the days when Daddy could discuss the events of the day with her, tuck her into bed, give her a gentle hug and a good night kiss on the forehead. She no longer trusts any man and freezes at his touch, hurting him deeply. Mom cannot understand all that has taken place and fears probing for details because she might trigger an outburst of anger and drive her daughter back to the street. Both parents feel helpless, unable to reach the child they love so much.

This child—which we rescued from the trick pad—experiences confusion about her identity as a sexual being. She asks herself, did she do what she did because, somewhere deep within her, she really is a slut?

We must remember that this child had never experienced a sexual encounter up to two weeks before being put in the pad. She had no opportunity to learn how men and women properly relate. "What is 'normal' sex?" she asks. Is what she experienced at the hands of men, many the same age as her father, what men and women do normally? How does she treat a date now who wants to hold her hand or kiss her? Do the conventional flirting and courtship rituals, that are so much a part of our growing up, hold some other meaning for her than for her date?

Over the next few years, the young girl will struggle to come to grips with her sense of worth and her values. Everything of significance in her previous life has been turned upside down on the street. In what relationships does she place her trust? She valued the closeness and friendship of a man who turned her out as a prostitute. Her parents failed to protect her from the seduction of the streets; the police rescued her and will bring her up on charges before the courts; social agencies will threaten to take her child; social workers will be too busy to help; therapists will blame rather than heal; and school friends will abandon her.

For twelve months, her pimp indoctrinated her with the idea that society's rules are outmoded, irrelevant, and made to be broken. Sex, she quickly learned, was a tool to exercise control over others, not a gesture of love and commitment. Money, as she learned on the street, isn't a medium of exchange, but rather a commodity to be flaunted, a measure of influence and power, a method of keeping score. Easily earned, and easily replaced, money on the street, as she grew to understand it, was a paradox: it is everything and it is nothing. She'd watched her pimp squander hundreds of thousands of dollars, oblivious to how she'd earned it or how quickly he spent it.

She maintained that the law works for other people, not for her. It could not protect or help her, only persecute her. Her parents, the counselors, medical people, and the police would use the law against her, to "bring her into line."

These were the values this damaged fifteen year old took with her that evening when we rescued her from the trick pad and transported to a recovery center.

That then, is the Game! The Life!

For the predator, the pimp, "the game" is an exciting and profitable pastime; for his prey—the child prostitute—"the life" is a struggle for her very existence.

8

Breaking Free

On the streets, I can get condoms, sandwiches, fresh needles, a drop-in centre
to sleep in, money from turning tricks, and friends to smoke up with.
How come I'm still lonely?

CHILD prostitution is a growth industry for the nineties. Once confined to areas such as Manila, Bangkok and Singapore, the prostitution of children is now a firmly established activity in both Canadian and U.S. cities. It is an industry we must understand before we can stop it. This chapter describes how a child becomes involved in prostitution, and how she may leave or be rescued from "the life."

Breaking free of the influence of both her pimp and the lifestyle can be a daunting task for a young girl. It is especially difficult for someone who has become deeply indoctrinated into believing that her fate is to live the life of a prostitute and that her pimp holds all power over her.

In order to fully comprehend the mechanisms needed to change the thought patterns that the girl has absorbed, we must examine the forces that brought her to the point of selling herself to strangers. While we know something of the various techniques used by pimps, it is important to understand how girls become vulnerable to their approaches.

Approaches and Methods of Recruiting

There are three common characteristics shared by the girls who become involved in prostitution. They have real or perceived fear or fears, a deep need for belonging, and issues surrounding their self-esteem. Preying on such girls, the pimps and predators hone in on one, two, or all three of these needs and, with seemingly little effort, turn ordinary young children into prostitutes.

One of two compulsions initiates any young girl's arrival on the street. They have been either running *from something* or *to something*.

They may be trying to escape from sexual, physical, or emotional abuse within the home, or from feelings of worthlessness, or from fear. They may also be trying to find a person, or group, who will accept them as they are.

In running to something, some youngsters believe that the streets are an exciting place: freedom from parental authority, and a never-ending series of parties, booze, drugs, stimulating friends, and fast times. They believe that pimps, dealers, and panners are "living on the edge" and have that special "something" that the mainstream world is missing.

Street outreach workers reveal that, once on the street for several months, a bizarre change in a girl's thought processes takes place. Girls feel safer on the streets than in a loving home. They feel more wanted and accepted by their "street family" than by anyone else in society. They also show a higher degree of self-esteem when on the run than when in therapy or in a secure, loving environment.

As difficult as this is for us to understand, we must accept this observation as reality. Failure to do so puts us at an enormous disadvantage when dealing with street issues.

Whatever the reason for leaving home, the streets become a trap. Nothing comes easily or free. In the 60s there was a popular bumper sticker. It read *Gas, Grass, or Ass—Nobody Rides For Free*. True to this conventional wisdom, there is always a price to pay—and prices on the streets are the dearest of all.

Seduction, coercion, even kidnapping, are the three methods a pimp uses to secure new "product" for his stable. Most pimps use only one of the methods, but we must remember that there are no rules. Sometimes he employs all three—in progressive stages—until he attains his goal.

Seduction

Seduction is the most common method used by pimps. Deceit, empty promises and the force of his personality are the tools he uses to persuade young women to subject themselves to his wishes and become prostitutes.

In order to achieve success using this method, he must seek out girls who are vulnerable to his approach. One pimp I interviewed had developed what he thought was a very effective system. He would walk through suburban shopping centers, paying particular attention to the mall's food courts. If he saw a young girl sitting alone, he would pass close by her table, brush against her chair, or draw her attention by any number of moves. When she looks at him, he gazes admiringly at her and compliments her on her hair.

It was at that point he conducted his preliminary assessment. If she politely thanked him, then turned her attention away from him, he would continue on his way. If, however, she fussed and patted her hair, and rejected his compliment by retorting, "Oh no, it's a mess," or "Yuk, it sucks...how can you say this is cool?" he would have his opening. He'd found a possible victim—one whose self-esteem was susceptible to a stranger's influence.

He may shower her with inexpensive, sentimental gifts. He may impress her with large rolls of money, with his "generosity," and with expensive-looking clothes. The pimp then sets to work to erode her connections with her family and her friends, readily supporting any idea that they both undervalue and fail to appreciate her. At the same time, he places himself in the position of being a primary friend, a confidant, and a protector. He begins seeking her trust and her affections and painting grandiose scenarios about their future together.

It's just a matter of time before she falls in love with him and willingly does anything he asks. His ruse is complete when he lures her into living with him or with his "friends."

Coercion

Coercion is another predatory method commonly used by a pimp. After running away from home—for any number of reasons—a young girl soon runs out of the resources to keep herself safe and alive. In order to obtain food, lodging, or drugs, she may resort to panhandling, or engage in sexual acts for money or shelter. Some girls commit petty crimes such as shoplifting. Eventually, despite her continual movements on the street, someone notices her.

The predator, learning of her presence and recognizing her susceptibility, aggressively approaches her. By this time, he's done a little homework and probably knows the names of her friends and where her family lives. Ultimately, and very quickly, he uses intimidation to force her into prostitution. He outright blackmails her with threats to inflict physical harm on her or her family, or to expose her sexual or criminal activities.

One particular Asian gang in the eastern United States specializes in this form of recruitment. They look for a young girl working off-track, engaged in selling sexual services in order to survive. They invite her for a ride in their car.

As soon as she is under their control, they tie her up, place a revolver in her mouth and "dry-fire" it several times. They make repeated threats to kill her and all her family members if she does not fall in line. Their terrorism almost always results in compliance. Helpless, horrified, intimidated, and fearful, she has little choice.

A pimp generally reserves the coercion method to obtain girls for trick-pad operations as opposed to on-street work. Because the pimp has the power to continually isolate her from her family and friends, he readily maintains a consistent level of intimidation. In order to make the terror real, the pimp will divest her of all personal belongings that often includes an address book listing the names, addresses and phone numbers of close friends and family members.

Stripped of all personal power and identity, many of these prostitutes simply "disappear."

Kidnapping

Although it garners headlines whenever it happens, kidnapping is the most infrequently used of the three methods. Generally, a pimp kidnaps girls already involved in prostitution. Kidnapping is also the most unreliable method because the pimp has no hold on the girl other than physical restraint. She requires constant supervision so that she will not escape, and therefore, the pimp needs either a permanent location to detain her, or a large number of accomplices to constantly monitor his prey.

Usually, a pimp resorts to kidnapping because he has a pressing need to add another girl to his stable. This need may arise through the demands of a particular customer, or from a battle between pimps, or for the prospect of quick profits in the underground sex film industry.

Not all kidnappings victimize prostitutes; some target potential prostitutes. For example, in a recent case in eastern Canada, investigators discovered that a mainstream pimp either seduced or coerced a number of young girls into working as prostitutes. His customers' demand for more product became intense, but he was not able to secure the number of young girls he required. Instead, he targeted and kidnapped several youngsters who had run away from home, but were not as yet working as prostitutes.

Forced to quickly recruit an extensive network of people to control his new acquisitions, the pimp's new accomplices proved unreliable. A weak spot soon developed in his organization. Taking advantage of an escape opportunity, one girl fled his influence and telephoned her mother. On the basis of her information, the police conducted a series of raids that located eight girls and returned them to their homes. The pimp's response? "I should have had more help to control them."

Breaking Free

How do these children break free from the cult-like grip of prostitution and escape from their pimps? Some walk away, some run away or are cast away, still others exit after the death of their pimp. In more direct interventions, some child prostitutes are "rescued" by parents or friends— a technique that seldom succeeds. Sometimes outsiders initiate rescues; sometimes the participants begin the process themselves. Still other rescues come about by random chance.

The Walk-Away

Sometimes a young prostitute simply decides one day that the game is not in her best interests, tells her pimp she's leaving, and returns home. This is a rare occurrence but it does happen. How does it happen? Somehow, the prostitute has retained enough self-determination and decision-making capacities to assess her situation, deal with various traumas, and think for herself. Girls and women who settle on a plan to walk away find the strength to face up to the pimp and leave "the life."

• • •

Kelly ran away from home, lured by the bright lights and loud music of city bars and clubs. Determined to stay in this environment, she prostituted herself the second night away from home. She believed that she could hit the streets the very next night and score some more easy money, but some of the older prostitutes hassled her ruthlessly—or as the street language puts it, they "jacked her up." This was a terrifying experience for her, and she would have left the stroll if she could have returned home. Instead, she determined she would survive on the streets and searched for a way to achieve her goal.

She made friends with one of the girls on the stroll who introduced Kelly to her pimp. Kelly worked for him for almost two years, but in time the enticements of the street faded. One night, Kelly returned from her shift and told her pimp she was quitting. He threatened to beat her as he'd done in the past, but she simply ignored him and walked out the door.

The Run-Away

This is probably the most common of all exit procedures. The prostitute comes to the conclusion that she wants out, but she's terrified that if her pimp discovers this decision, he will inflict a beating or, in extreme cases, kill her. Usually, an experience with a violent customer is behind her decision. She realizes how close to the edge of death she walks every day. Sometimes an episode with her pimp forces her decision. Perhaps he's meted out a severe beating, sold her baby, or replaced her as his "main."

• • •

Running from an abusive home, Amber was quickly seduced into the life. Conned by the rap from an experienced pimp, she remained in the game for almost three years. On two occasions, she tried to negotiate a leaving fee with her pimp, but to no avail. On the third try, she stashed a few hundred dollars from an evening's work, took a taxi to the airport and moved to another city.

• • •

Sometimes the runaway succeeds in leaving "the game"; sometimes she's pursued, punished and, either returned to the pimp's stable, sold—or maybe even killed. Other times, another pimp spots her as a runaway and she's trapped into "the life" once again. Whatever the outcome, her initial flight is dogged by fear and fueled by courage.

The Cast-Away

A prostitute is castaway or released from a pimp's control by the pimp. This happens when she becomes too much of a problem for a pimp and, by keeping her he loses the respect of other players in the game. The prostitute may be cast away if she becomes disabled, disfigured, or if she develops AIDS, Hepatitis B, or a drug addiction where the cost of her habit equals or exceeds her income as a working prostitute. Some players refer to these prostitutes as "the walking dead."

Leaving is seldom her choice and the pimp frequently drives her out of his stable and away from the stroll. Basically, she's left to fend for herself. This almost never occurs to young girls, because of their high value in the trade. It does, however, occur fairly regularly among prostitutes in their late twenties or older. Few survive after being cast out.

• • •

Mattie became a prostitute at the age of eleven. Within a year she started using marijuana and hash regularly. By fourteen she was into cocaine, and by fifteen she was mainlining heroin. She existed only for the next fix. Try as he would, her pimp could not get her to reduce her drug dependencies, and when her habit grew to over $1,000 a day, he tossed her away. A few months later, Mattie was found dead in a hotel parking lot; she was twenty years old.

Death of the Pimp

Like the cast away, the death of a pimp has only a temporary effect on a young prostitute. Likely, a new pimp will bump her almost immediately. An older prostitute, however, may find a window of opportunity to leave the life after her pimp's death. Probably she worked for the now-deceased pimp for a number of years and, although her value to him may have steadily declined, he kept her to service a select number of clients. His death would eliminate that particular market. In the ensuing confusion of his death there may be little call on her time from her regular clients. She may seize the chance to leave the game.

• • •

Ardella had been a prostitute for seven years when a customer took a razor to her face. When she did not go to a hospital for treatment, her lacerations became infected, leaving large ugly scars. Her upper lip was so badly cut that, when it healed, it appeared as if she had a cleft palate. She now had limited value on the street; but instead of casting her away, her pimp marketed Ardella to a small group of sado-masochists. They continued to heap abuse and torture upon her.

When police killed her pimp in a shootout, Ardella had no one to turn to, nor any money to survive. She went back out onto the street but could not compete on the regular strolls. Desperate, she contacted the Salvation Army; through them, she exited the street.

Parental Rescue

Often, concerned parents and friends first employ this technique to rescue a child from the streets. In this approach, the rescuers spot the youngster, track her to a location and "kidnap" her from the pimp. Knowledgeable people rarely employ this method, as it is seldom successful, but enough completions take place to warrant mentioning it.

• • •

Robin was only on the street for a week when her mother mounted an extensive campaign to get her back. In spite of all the resources brought to her disposal, including Children's Aid, Youth Court, and the police, she was unable to rescue her daughter. Frustrated with the system, she went undercover herself, posing as an old prostitute. Frequenting the bars and hang-outs around the stroll, she eventually learned the identity of the pimp who was running her child and where he was keeping her.

Aided by five robust male friends, the mother forced open the door of the apartment and, holding a gun on the pimp, took Robin back.

Exit Counseled

This is now becoming the most effective method of extracting a child from the life. In the process of exit counseling, an outreach worker makes contact with a young prostitute. Over the course of days, weeks, or even months, she establishes a relationship with the girl that ultimately leads to the girl willingly leaving the control of her pimp. The exit counselor, with the help of a team of specialists, helps her reestablish contact with mainstream society.

• • •

Anna had worked on the street for two and a half years. During the last four months of her involvement, she met an outreach worker from a social agency. They became friends and a trust formed between them. Anna became increasingly dependent on the worker's advice and support.

The counselor did not make promises she was unable or unwilling to keep. Their relationship grew and eventually Anna revealed to the counselor that she was ready to leave the life. The counselor made preparations for a recovery center to accept Anna along with her small son whom she loved dearly.

The evening came, and the counselor picked her up on the stroll with her child. She has never returned.

The Team Approach

In whatever manner the young girl exits the world of prostitution, it is important to bear in mind that, unless the environment that she originally came from is modified, the chances of her slipping back into the life are both very real and probable. Not only must the previous circumstances change, there must be full preparations made for her return.

It is all but impossible for parents or guardians to accomplish on their own. They must gather a team around them, a team with expertise in these matters, who can assist in bringing the child back safely. The members of the team work in concert and they operate from knowledge based on understanding "the game."

This collaboration may include, in addition to the parents: a therapist trained in either cults, sexual slavery, or prostitution (the similarities are striking), a police officer knowledgeable about street issues, an exit counselor who has worked with young women trapped in the life, and a medical professional, usually a physician. Although not necessarily a part of the front-line team, a lawyer consults with the team and deals with some of the peripheral issues that arise when the child has been removed from the street. Each part of the team—the parents or guardians, the police officer, the exit counselor or outreach worker, the medical professional or physician, and the lawyer—bring a special qualification, talent or knowledge base to the team.

The Parents

The parents are the most crucial members of the team. They have the greatest motivation, the most urgency and the most love. I have used the word "parents" as a generic term for a role filled by the child's biological or adoptive parents or her guardians. Because neither the parents nor guardians may be available to some children, I have extended the term to cover the person or persons I have come to describe as a "connector"—a relative (grandparent, aunt, or uncle, etc.) or a friend of the family. This person has been in a positive relationship with the child and earnestly seeks that child's well being.

Parents, guardians, or connectors can also be the most destructive element on the team because their emotions may overrun the team's planning and jeopardize the entire effort. Sometimes, they may make decisions based, not on logic, but on their emotional responses of anger, love, concern, or fear.

The team understands, from the outset, that the parents usually know their daughter at a deeper level than they do or than the pimp does. Her parents know her deepest fears, her secret dreams, her social aspirations, and her passions. They also know what pleases her: the relative she idolizes, the subject she most enjoys in school, her best sports activity, and her favorite book. The pimp knows none of these "hot buttons." So, when the campaign gets underway, he finds himself at a disadvantage, perhaps for the first time in his life.

Mom and Dad must realize that they are in a war—a battle for the life of their daughter! The team's preparation of the parents for that struggle becomes, perhaps, the most important—yet most overlooked—aspect of the entire process. They must be prepared to never let go, to resist backing down for even a moment, to avoid becoming discouraged or disheartened, or giving up when the going gets rough, as it surely will.

Because the parents most often are the ones who have the greatest concern, it is up to them to get the campaign underway. They are the ones who will seek out and bring onto the team those who can help them win back their child. To assemble the team, they must conduct their own investigations—not to gather evidence to put the pimp in jail—but searches into the backgrounds and abilities of those they ask to assist. Once they've recruited the members of the team, the parent's job begins in earnest as they coordinate with the team, learn from and accept advice from them, and offer every assistance to them.

Police Officer

The police officer brings a professional objectivity to the recovery effort. He or she arrives on the team with a mostly altruistic interest, without hidden agendas, other that to see that the "bad guy" eventually goes to prison. As an investigator in the child's case, the officer commits to engage the department's resources and search mechanisms. He or she expresses a willingness to go to court and to testify as an expert witness. Essentially, the officer forms a wall of protection around the victim by bringing a full combat team—the entire police force—to the battle.

The officer's job is multidimensional. He or she brings to the team an extensive knowledge about prostitution and about the local sex trade. As a facilitator, the officer uses his or her experience to educate the parents about the game, illustrating hard data with anecdotal evidence. Dealing with the frustration levels of the parents has become a special skill for this officer.

The officer brings extensive expertise to the team of how the prostitution game operates. Knowledge about the local pimps, who controls what streets and corners, locations of the various "live" clubs, and who frequents them, becomes essential information for the team. He or she knows what nights are "ladies' nights" at the clubs, and what doormen accept "tips" to allow underage females inside. The officer must have connections within the live community, as well as personal sources in other police agencies to assist in tracking both the pimp and the prostitute.

The police officer instructs the parents to build a file that contains much more than the standard pictures and details of their daughter. It lists every friend that they know about, copies of all phone bills prior to the date she left, and highlights any collect calls made since her disappearance. The parents must search through their daughter's old school papers, letters, notes, and diaries, and provide photocopies of all official records. The officer impresses on the parents to record all information, no matter how minor, in the investigative folder, for a single piece of data may be the key to locating her.

The officer guides the parents in the process to list their child as missing. With this status the police may apprehend the child if she surfaces during a raid or sting operation. The parents should also list her as a missing person with all agencies that record children who have run away or been kidnapped.

The team relies on this officer's experience to design the essential safety factors surrounding the operation. In effect, these are the ground rules for each specific case and every team member—including the parents—must agree to respect these boundaries. A child's life is at stake.

Exit Counselor

The exit counselor, like the police officer, has extensive knowledge of prostitution. Her knowledge, however, focuses primarily on the pimp-prostitute relationship and the hold that the predator has over the girl. Sometimes, the counselor's personal experience augments her training and understanding; she may have been a prostitute herself and successfully made a full recovery. Outreach workers are invaluable to the team and to the child because she speaks to the girl from a far different position than the parents, the police or any other "authority" figures.

With her extensive street experience, the exit counselor becomes a primary figure in the outreach effort. Her significant knowledge of street language and culture forms a critical basis of communication with the young girl.

She inspires confidence in the victims because she has been on the streets and knows the scene. She works on the premise that she must earn the honor of a child prostitute's trust, rather than have the child earn her trust. Her efforts are eventually rewarded. With her colleagues, she nurtures the child's healthy dependency on her and the outreach team. She is a source of support and information for the child. Sometimes she works as a mediator between the child and others in the "straight world" or those on the team. Sometimes she's just a very good listener.

The exit counselor also uses her currency with "the system" to pinpoint and tap into various social agencies, business associations, service clubs and professional resources to respond to the demands of individual cases. She speaks to them with authority, fluent in their missions and in their abilities to assist in the intervention and recovery processes. She brings analysis to the situation and provides feedback, support, and supervision to the other workers on the team.

A seasoned and experienced worker, the exit counselor effectively works "both sides" of the street. She's a chameleon-like character, moving from one culture to another and mediating between the two in order to facilitate the changes necessary to bring a youngster off the street and back into a healthy life.

Medical Professional

The medical professional on the team is usually a physician and frequently that doctor represents the whole staff of a medical office. Their task is to be ready for the potential medical problems the child may exhibit when she leaves the street. These may include any number of sexually transmitted diseases, skin disorders, and infections, intestinal parasites, body lice, reproductive tract dysfunction, malnutrition, and drug or alcohol addiction. The child may be pregnant. The doctor and her medical team should be sensitive to other severe medical problems arising from massive and extensive sexual abuse. For example, the child may have suffered colon or bowel damage from repeated anal rapes or have gonorrhea of the mouth and throat.

Another part of their task is to expose the team—especially the parents—to the range of medical problems the child may have after exiting the street. In return, the team should receive disclosure of a full and frank discussion between the parents and their family doctor. The team recognizes that it is more important that the physician establish the right "fit" with the child than with the parents.

The parents assist by making arrangements to update the young girl's medical records and have them available at short notice. They also bring her medical insurer on-line so that if all her papers are missing, she can receive treatment with a minimum of delay. The medical clinic should create a file and have it readily available. Quite often, the clinic's receptionists and other front line workers are briefed on the file and code it for immediate and special attention for when the child visits.

The physician is usually a female who understands victimology and a child's fear of medical professionals as part of the larger "straight" world. The physician and her staff are willing to take time to build a rapport with the child, ease her fears and increase her comfort levels. Their goal is to inspire her confidence to the point that the child will assist proactively in her own treatment and recovery.

To reach this goal, the physician and her staff develop a gentle approach to the child. They anticipate the youngster's first visit may be a simple "drop-in" without an appointment. At that time, alerted to her potential visit, they have a chart ready and an "instant" time slot for the doctor to see the child.

Her anxieties about the visit become less when she knows she doesn't have to wait an interminable time in the waiting room. During the first visit, which focuses on building trust in the child, her comfort level increases as the physician gently explores her medical condition through conversation and observation.

The physician arranges a second visit and eventually a series of visits as the child's trust level increases. The child, who may have an attention deficit, experiences little waiting and no pressure from the physician or her staff. With each visit, the treatment likely becomes more serious and exams may become more invasive, but everything is done with the child's understanding and full consent. The child becomes aware that she controls her own health care. This marks one of the first times in a long time that she has had control over any part of her life.

Lawyer

With rare exceptions, there are almost always a number of legal issues that the team must address when a child exits the life of prostitution.

Because of the very nature of the activity, the child has usually been a part of peripheral criminal activities including thefts, drugs, assaults and frauds. Some charges will stem from the system rather than from the street. The child could, for example, face charges of "breach of conduct" or "escape from lawful custody."

The lawyer forms an essential part of the team. Knowledgeable in the area of child welfare legislation, a lawyer supplies the team with the legal ramifications of the case. The team will need to know what rights parents have as well as the rights of the child. The counsel sets aside much of the adversarial role he or she normally plays and focuses instead on the good of the child.

The lawyer seeks to deal with all charges in the most expeditious manner so that the healing process can begin for the child. If the court sentences the child to a period of incarceration, then the lawyer must abide by the wishes of the parents and ask for the appropriate court provisions. Too often, the lawyer fights to have the child unconditionally released from all charges. While on the surface, this may seem advantageous to the case, removing the child's responsibility for breaking the law can be crippling to her eventual recovery.

Instead, the lawyer must be ready to persuade a judge to issue an order of secure treatment. Often that means having to convince the court of the child's inability, at this stage and in her condition, to make rational decisions on her own. The other partners in the team will assist the lawyer in presenting a well-rounded case with their expert testimony.

What about civil litigation against the pimp for the devastating effect he had on the child? The lawyer should also explore this avenue, even though pimps seldom have any significant assets. In recent years, however, there have been several successful lawsuits in which families of victims obtained judgments against the pimp. In one civil proceeding the court seized a new Corvette, in another a house, and in a third case, the pimp's bank account was seized.

As a protector of the child, the lawyer may seek restraining orders against the pimp or pursue a paternity claim. Because pimps generally shun the exposure of daylight court, most of these legal actions are quickly resolved to the team's satisfaction.

In the legal activities surrounding the child and her family, the lawyer maintains a professional confidence. Without divulging personal information, a lawyer may advise and support the other members of the team by alerting them to potential problems. In all legal consultations, the lawyer strives to make the child part of the picture.

The Therapist

A child coming off the street and out of prostitution needs therapeutic attention as much as she needs medical attention—and just as quickly. The therapist on the team fills a critical role in the intervention and recovery processes as she briefs the team well in advance about the emotional, spiritual, and behavioral damage a child suffers as a result of involvement in prostitution. Like the physician, the attending therapist is usually a woman, principally because the child will be more comfortable with a professional of the same gender.

The therapist is a specialist in treating the victims of sexual abuse and prostitution. In particular, she has experience in the assessment and counseling of abused children. Her expertise, however, is even more specialized, and therein lies her value to the child and the team. She is also an expert in the analysis of sexual slavery and cult behaviors. While there are scores of dedicated therapists experienced in dealing with sexual abuse, only a handful have studied the phenomena of sexual slavery and cults.

Many times, the team locates specialized therapists through sexual assault centers or through the local police Vice Squad. In every major city there are private organizations that deal with prostitution and recovering prostitutes, and many have such therapists on retainer.

With her particular perspectives, this therapist can successfully treat a child rescued from prostitution. She understands that in the first two to three weeks, this child may be full of guilt for leaving the life—for leaving behind her friends and even her pimp. Understanding that the life has conditioned the child to accept guilt as part of her life on the streets, the therapist gently and slowly reaches back into the child's life, searching for other sources of guilt or hurt. Her work, ironically, is not unlike the therapy that treats women who display the battered wife syndrome. By not going back in too far or too fast, the therapist soon begins to assist in the child's healing process.

The Intervention Process

The team approach addresses the dual problem of rescuing the child prostitute: first the difficult removal process of the child from the street, and second, the healing and restoration of the child to family, society, and to a viable future. In this chapter, I've explored the educational process that every team must participate in to learn *what* we are fighting. Only after understanding how and why children become prostitutes can we effectively fight for children caught in "the game."

It's one thing to discuss the needs and activities of the team as an academic exercise. It is quite another to have a specific plan of action, and to see the intervention process through to its desired conclusion—the safe return of the child.

Before the team implements any plan, they must locate the youngster. The police officer on the team usually provides this key information. When the team knows the locations—where she stays and those she frequents—they naturally want to take immediate action. If the young girl's life is not in immediate danger, however, it is often a wiser course of action to proceed through a number of proven steps.

The team knows that the probability of success for a young prostitute to not only come off the street but to remain off the street, corresponds to the degree of motivation that comes from the child herself. As their first goal, the team makes contact with the child through the exit counselor.

She gradually initiates conversations with the child, always conscious of the need to meet the youngster on her own terms. The counselor does not demand, threaten, or impose on the girl, but gradually builds a base of trust. Knowing that she will be "tested" the counselor does not make promises that she cannot fulfil.

Over time the counselor enhances the trusting relationship with the young prostitute and slowly begins to replace the negative dependent relationship the child has with her pimp. Through conversation and skilled observation, the counselor assesses the child's emergency needs and makes referrals to a network of local social service agencies and hospitals. Through her knowledge of other agencies and organizations, and with her reputation, the counselor has the ability to contact these resources and quickly cut through "red tape." She may provide the child with transportation to health services or shelters, offer food or clothing to her, or supply information about health care and hygiene.

As their relationship develops, the counselor begins to talk more aggressively with the child about leaving the streets and reconnecting to the straight life. She discusses alternatives with the youngster, including independent living, returning home, or entering a residential treatment program. Though her ultimate goal is to see the child leave prostitution, the counselor works at the child's own pace. As always, the team works behind the scenes, ready for the moment the child decides to leave the street.

The following chart summarizes the intervention process and describes the child's condition, her characteristic responses to the team, the team's goals, and the anticipated timelines to complete the process. While each child's case is unique, it is fairly typical for her to experience these three steps before she can break free.

Child prostitution has many dimensions. The team approach assembles a group of specialists to respond to this multi-dimensional problem. They become a collaborative group with the responsibility to create a plan that not only brings the child back safely, but brings her back permanently.

The team's collective talents contribute to initiating the intervention process long before the child prostitute reaches the point of breaking free from the exploitative situation that has trapped her. Once they build the trusting relationship so necessary in helping the girl escape the street and her pimp, their next step is to begin the recovery process.

Whereas the rescue or intervention process can take days or months or even a full year, the recovery process typically requires three or more years. After breaking free, the child must receive the team's support and assistance in her long journey home.

Chart 1: Stages in the Intervention Process.

Stage	Condition / Goal / Timeline	Behavior:
I	**Condition**: *Controlled* **Goal**: *to decrease:* • distrust • defensiveness **Timeline**: *1 day – several weeks*	Controlled by her pimp, drugs, or by the street itself, her behavior ranges from indifference to outright hostility. She often becomes short in her responses when attempts are made to engage her in conversation.
II	**Condition**: *Contacted* **Goal**: *to increase:* • trust • testing **Timeline**: *1 – 6 months*	Contacted by an outreach worker, a safe friend, or a former prostitute employed as a team member, she will accept a "hello," then gradually, as trust builds, she will accept coffee, a meal, cigarettes, or a "favor" such as a ride. She starts to feel worthy of attention and begins to understand the counselor is really there "for her." She'll look for opportunities to test the validity of the person's promises.
III	**Condition**: *Convinced* **Goal**: *to enhance:* • respect • relationships **Timeline**: *3 – 12 months*	Convinced that the counselor is working in her best interests, she desires more contact. She will initiate contact with the designated person to assist in solving problems. When she accepts stated boundaries, she strives to achieve them. She trusts the "word" of the counselor and wants her to be involved in her life. She'll move home or to a recovery centre if the counselor facilitates the process.

9

Coming Home

I've had four dads, nine social workers, three probation officers, sixteen addresses, eleven schools, thirteen step brothers and sisters, four group homes, six foster homes, and five therapists. And you're upset because I don't seem to be connecting very well?

FORMING the team and bringing the young girl out of "the game"— the intervention process—sets the stage for the most critical step of all: coming home. The team has been working together through the intervention process. They undergo more briefings to be ready for her after she exits the street. We call this next stage "the recovery process." It is the final step in bringing her out of "the life."

People who work extensively with recovering child prostitutes find that there are three factors that must be present for the recovery process to succeed. First, the child must feel the necessary supports and resources are in place that are external to herself. These include:

- trusting relationships
- access to legal, health, educational, social, welfare and security services
- emotional support outside the family
- structure and rules
- adult encouragement to be autonomous
- stable environment
- role models
- moral leadership
- people around who love unconditionally
- adults who can set reasonable limits for the child
- adults who take a leadership role
- adults who can be counted on to deliver help when needed

Second, the child must develop personal internal strengths. These are:

- sense of being lovable
- autonomy
- appealing temperament

- achievement oriented
- self-esteem
- a spiritual balance—belief in a higher power
- altruism
- focus on control of emotions

Finally, the child must have the opportunity to develop and achieve growth in these social and interpersonal skills:
- creativity
- persistence
- humor
- communications
- problem solving
- impulse control
- trusting relationships
- social skills
- intellectual skills

The list seems like a tall order. The team knows that they must allocate a substantial amount of time, money and resources to the recovery process.

And now for the good news.

In spite of the almost overwhelming task that the team faces, their success rate in restoring a child prostitute to society is outstanding. If the caring adults involved refuse to give up the fight and hang on against intimidating odds, chances are the child can be, and will be, taken back.

In almost every case of failure, we can trace the root cause to one of the adults (usually a parent) giving up. Some people cannot continue their involvement because of burnout, stress, anger and resentment. This is understandable. The effort required to combat the lure of the streets and to break the hold a pimp has over a prostitute can exhaust even the most dedicated person. That is a primary reason why the team approach is optimal. Almost every successfully concluded case has, at its core, a talented and dedicated group of individuals determined to succeed.

In this chapter I discuss the recovery process and its techniques. In the second part of this chapter, I relate several stories of girls who "made it out of the life," and are now working at regular jobs, raising families, and putting their lives back together. These are true stories, about real people. They illustrate the success of the team approach.

What happens when the girls reunite with their families or enter foster care or treatment facilities? Not only must the techniques used to bring them off the street be maintained but there must be growth in their lives as they accept and adopt a protection system that will allow them to build a new life and to resist the lure of the streets in the future.

Preparing For Arrival

Once the team assembles, develops the files and begins their investigations, they quickly begin to address some of the practical issues. After the child leaves prostitution, where and how will she live? What financial and educational arrangements will she require? How will the family handle her re-entry into the home and into their social group? What does she require to re-learn about a "normal" life, and who will be in charge of this socialization process? What are her special issues concerning trust; will she learn to believe once again in cultural norms, practices, and institutions?

The goal of the recovery process is to aid the child in making a successful transition from street life to healthy independence. Part of the process involves teaching her basic, but important living skills that will help her live a productive, independent life. Ideally, the process helps the child return home—if and when that is feasible.

The move from "the street to the straight" is one made up of small, yet identifiable steps. In order to reach a goal, we must know what the goal is. We must also be aware of the steps needed to achieve the goal. The following chart explains the five stages a child typically moves through in the recovery process. Each stage marks her progress away from the street and closer to achieving a successful reintegration with mainstream society.

In preparing for her arrival, the team needs to understand the characteristic behaviours and anticipate the time lines for each stage in the recovery process. While there is no "typical" victim, we can anticipate—based on both experience as well as anecdotal evidence—the following conditions, characteristics, and time lines.

Chart 2: Stages in the Integration Process.

Stage	Condition / Goal	Behavior
I	**Condition**: *Dissociated* **Goal**: *Decrease*: • distress • detatchment • denial • defensiveness **Timeline**: *up to 3 months*	**Behavior**: She has feelings of helplessness, fearfulness, and of being overwhelmed by life. She feels a lack of control over the future. Emotionally disturbed, she adjusts poorly. She may go through a "honeymoon" period, and will "crash" at the 3 day, 3 week, or 3 month mark. This is normal.
II	**Condition**: *Early Integration* **Goal**: *Enhance Empowering Ideas* • I am • I can • I have • I will **Timeline**: *6 – 12 months*	She feels welcomed, loved and accepted. She participates in group discussions, shares responsibilities, and accepts discipline because "it's in my interest." When corrected and held accountable for her actions, she acknowledges she is important and that people care about her. Realizing that this is not "just another placement," she takes increasing pride in her accomplishments and those of others in the "family." She more readily accepts discipline and boundaries without running away.
III	**Condition**: *Creative* **Goal**: *Increase*: • choices • connectiveness **Timeline**: *12 – 18 months*	She experiences the beauty of a loving environment, good health, safety, and friendship. She begins to make choices that connect with all the significant characteristics of a responsible life. Gradually her gentleness emerges. Choices become increasingly well-thought out. She begins volunteer work, church activities and pastimes that are both healthy and self-initiated.
IV	**Condition**: *Stabilizing* **Goal**: *Promote*: • health • harmony **Timeline**: *18 – 24 months*	She accepts some setbacks without it affecting her unnecessarily. She handles new challenges, makes good decisions about finances, nutrition and associates. We see some real stability in her life as she assumes significant responsibilities and completes self-initiated projects.
V	**Condition**: *Integrated* **Goal**: *Sustain*: • belief • balance • benefits **Timeline**: *24 – 36 months*	She gradually gains full independence from the center. Fully independent, she maintains a "normal" lifestyle, engaging in standard pursuits in the "straight" world. She moves toward independent living and requires only occasional support—like any child in a standard family structure.

In reviewing the chart, remember that each child requires a highly individualized program. Children come from all sorts of backgrounds, have widely differing needs and are of different ages—both chronologically and developmentally. Most children, however, will pass through these five stages. It is also important to understand that children will move back and forth between present and previous stages. However, she will seldom, if ever, slip back by more than one stage.

The child's development in Stages II through IV evolves concurrently, and the foundation for Stage V is being laid from the very beginning of the recovery process.

Living Arrangements

When the child returns home or to a recovery center, she feels disoriented and disconnected. In her mind, she may think she's exchanged one hostile situation for another. She's grown accustomed to mistrusting almost everyone and everything—including her own emotions. On the street she learned to surrender control and not to question manipulation by peers and pimps.

The first four to eight weeks are critical. In that time the child typically tests the unfamiliar boundaries of the new living situation. The parents or guardians have probably obtained legal control over her life. At first, she may resent their power, resist all discipline as an imposition on her personal freedom, and display an inordinate amount of anger. Her temper may have a short fuse. Her frustration often peaks because she perceives the streets as an easier environment in which to live than living with the rules of her new life.

The youngster may describe life on the streets (even under the control of a pimp) as complete freedom compared to the constraints of a home. She will probably rebel, and sometimes even attempt to return to the streets or to use drugs and alcohol. Working a "regular" job for minimum wages is also difficult for someone who made significantly more money on the streets, even though she did not keep any of the money she earned.

People living in the same household with her may find the first few weeks uncomfortable, if not down right impossible.

Household members will have to adjust to a child that may appear more of a stranger than a loved one. Sometimes adjusting is a matter of perspective. Taking into account that a child who has been on the street from age thirteen to fifteen has spent 20% of her life in a subculture of degradation and violence, we may discover new levels of tolerance within ourselves.

She will need to re-learn the process of internal and external discipline. The young girl has become nocturnal. She's learned to live at night and sleep during the day. Who will be there for her and assist in adjusting her internal clock? Parents may have to teach her how to use an alarm clock and household appliances.

She may also exhibit other behaviors that appear irrational. For example, she may hoard food, hide possessions, insist that her bedroom door have a lock, sleep with all the lights in the room blazing, and have her "street clothes" packed and ready to go in a backpack. She may require coaching in fundamental issues of propriety and need to re-learn acceptable social norms for her behavior.

If she has moved home, other family members' routines and habits will also have to change. Males—especially fathers—will have to be careful about their appearance and refrain from appearing partially clothed within her sight. Males may find it difficult to be in her company in the face of her aversion to or even her outright rejection of all male–female encounters. Fathers, in particular, must set modelling norms for correct behavior.

Some of her reactions are habits, some are testing behaviors, while some reveal an inability to judge the scale and impact of her actions. She probably smokes heavily. She may express outrageous moral views and pepper her language with obscenities. The first task of the recovery team is to enable her to learn healthy habits for successful living. Every child progresses through this stage—and all other stages—at her own pace. The team should not set time limits for her to achieve her goals.

Financial Arrangements

The recovery process is expensive. Parents or guardians have already incurred the expense of removing her from the streets—that may have meant paying for travel costs from another city or even another country. Their financial commitment, however, is just beginning.

The family should anticipate countless drains on their budget. As soon as the child arrives from the street, they must begin asking critical questions. Does she have outstanding legal fines? Can her representatives persuade the courts to seek legal alternatives to monetary penalties by pursuing other avenues such as probation orders? What costs will the family face for a year or more of services from a lawyer, a therapist, and a physician? Will they encounter additional recovery costs such as fees for addiction centers, treatment facilities, or specialized foster care? What help can they expect from medical insurance plans, Children's Aid, and Legal Aid?

Whatever the living arrangement, within days after leaving the street, the child must undergo a complete medical assessment, which includes drug and AIDS testing, a dental examination, and a nutritional evaluation to determine her existing medical conditions and the need for immediate or long-term medical care.

The immediate financial commitment to the child can be substantial. She will need a whole new wardrobe. She may require remedial classes, or drug or alcohol counseling, vocational or life skills training, and medical attention not covered by health plans.

Parents often end up making decisions that generate significant costs. Sometimes they have the time to chart their expenses, but frequently situations arise where decisions must be made quickly, out of urgent necessity or through deeply felt compulsions. For example, they may have to make structural modifications to the family home. New living arrangements could bring new construction requirements, or the alteration of existing security or communication services. In a household where the mother works, she may feel compelled to take a leave of absence or quit her job. The family may need to hire extra people to assist with the care of other children or with household chores. Some families will opt to relocate to another city, move to a rural setting or even to another country.

Extraordinary financial commitments however, do not mean financial ruin. While every case brings individual demands and constraints, one of the added benefits of including the Exit Counselor is her knowledgeable and skilled access to a wide base of resources. Often business associations, service clubs, churches, and community organizations are willing and quick to respond to requests for monetary or material assistance. Many of these groups contribute silently, without fanfare or recognition.

Educational Arrangements

In all likelihood, the youngster has fallen behind her peers by two grades. Research has shown us that when girls coming off the street are immediately re-enrolled in a regular school, they experience nearly a 100% failure rate. Why does this happen?

First of all, the child has great difficulty in sitting through six or seven hours of schooling; sitting quietly is no longer one of her strong suites. She needs to learn how to relax in a new social situation where she may be a stranger, or where her street past may be well-known to her classmates. Her self-esteem issues become compounded and magnified by the school where she faces continual demands to demonstrate self-discipline and self-motivation. Should she make the attempt to return to a regular school and fail, she will experience a period of depression that could prove disastrous to her recovery.

The team, lead by the Exit Counselor, should make arrangements to have her enrolled in a special program or school that can deal with the characteristics of inattention, boredom, and cognitive difficulties. Ideally the child is placed in an alternative school, or if the circumstances dictate, within a secure residential school facility. Typically, the child re-enters school below the grade level of her peers. There she meets with fewer self-esteem issues and fewer awkward questions. Sometimes her schooling begins with tutors; in-home support workers may augment the tutors. With either approach, the outcome is predictably more successful. Usually the child regains the educational level of her peers; frequently she comes out ahead in the class standings.

Social Reintegration

The recovery process includes helping the child recover her position within mainstream culture. She is, after all, returning as a very different person from the one she was before she entered "the life." Full social reintegration can only take place when we understand the child prostitute as a victim—society's failure to recognize the nature of her victimization will only make her a victim a second time.

What does social reintegration mean? We have only to keep in mind the child and imagine her dilemmas in encountering the straight world. What does she say to former friends, relatives and acquaintances when they ask her where she was for the last year? How does she explain her absence? Will her language, appearance, or behavior offend them? Will she be welcome in the homes of her friends or in the homes of family friends? Can she expect former employers to hire her again? How will she react when a young man asks her for a date? How will she handle the flirting and courting rituals that are a part of every teenager's life?

It may help to remind ourselves that she is going through an accelerated learning curve. For a year or more, her socialization into our society's cultural norms has become perverted and stunted. She has as much to unlearn as she has to learn. Divorced from her own memories and emotions for a long period of her short life, she has much catching up to do.

As she reconnects with her own sense of self-determination and achievement, she frequently combats faulty perceptions imposed by others. She's not merely picking up where she left off in her life before prostitution; she's reconstructing, sometimes re-inventing herself. She's trying to develop all those skills, responses, expectations, and dreams that months or years in prostitution repressed in her normal social development.

Our job, as members of the mainstream culture, should be to assist in this part of her recovery process by supporting, teaching, and mentoring her. Anything less would amount to re-victimizing her.

Restructuring

Coming home means the child will have to begin mastering fundamental living skills. Sometimes she requires a re-orientation to "straight" life, but often she must acquire essential habits and abilities for the first time. For example, in "the life" she either lost or never had the chance to attain a sense of time or competency in handling money.

The team must make a decision about who is going have the task of teaching her to use an alarm clock. They might ask who will assist in developing punctuality and the use of calendars and notebooks. They need to anticipate the potential difficulties in meting out an allowance or in sending her on simple purchasing errands when she has lost all concept of the value of money.

In addition to learning the practical side of life skills, she must also re-orient or restructure her behavioral and emotional responses. Who will help her learn appropriate dress codes and makeup application? Where and when can she smoke cigarettes? She must develop strategies for anger or frustration management, but she can't always do this on her own. Where can she obtain this competence?

After her recent experiences, any family expecting this child to return to old pastimes and recreation is being unrealistic. Typically, the excitement she felt in her past leisure activities never matched the adrenaline rushes she knew on the street. Families will find greater success in connecting her with an exciting peer group—such as a skydiving club, a horseback drill team, or a performance troupe—than attempting to resurrect her interest in bowling, doll collecting, or bird watching. Eventually she may return to her old activities as the team assists her discovery of personality-centered rather than activity-centered recreation.

Restructuring, as part of the recovery process, is *the* essential component in restoring her ability to master essential life skills. It provides her with a foundation for addressing the myriad of challenges she faces in coming home.

Establishing Trust

Through her indoctrination on the street, the child prostitute believes that men and women in positions of authority cannot be trusted. Perhaps, for most of her life she has suffered one betrayal after another. Ironically, she may feel that she too has betrayed trust, especially the trust of those friends she's left behind in "the life."

We can understand how this child has lost trust in people. Even before leaving for a life on the street, and most definitely while living a street life, she has been used as a sexual object by all manner of men—many similar in age and occupation to that of her father, or her doctor, therapist or pastor. How can she trust any man ever again? Though she may hate men, she doesn't necessarily fear them or avoid them. Instead, she copes; she finds mechanisms, however inappropriate, for self-protection. Having learned that she has the ability to manipulate men through sexual contact—"to john" them—she's forgotten or discarded boundaries that should have never been broken. How will that trust and those boundaries be re-established?

While establishing new boundaries and re-confirming her trust by displaying sexual neutrality, fathers and other males close to her must strive to avoid giving her mixed signals by establishing clear boundaries. She may test re-established boundaries by displaying inappropriate behavior. In time she will respond positively to reconstructing new boundaries and begin to feel safe enough to trust them.

Part of her problem in establishing trust is learning to trust herself. A critical step she must make is to recognize that change must start from within herself and flow to the outside. She has to change fundamental ideas about her body image, about her self-worth, about her responsibilities, and about her abilities. She has to learn to trust other people, not only those in authority, but in herself and her future. The intervention and recovery team approach this idea by saying to the child, "Let us earn *your* trust," rather than insisting that she earn their trust or their acceptance. In this way the youngster witnesses a model for taking responsibility for owning trust.

Success Stories

The recovery process takes time and often comes at great cost. For the team members and especially for the child, success may seem elusive, but through the team approach, much dedication, and extremely hard work, they will reach the goal. In a process where patience is a virtue that is sometimes stretched thin, the participants have time on their side, for time can accommodate the tiny steps to recovery and nurture healing changes.

The following stories illustrate only five out of the hundreds of successes attributable to the team approach that follows this model of intervention and recovery. Many of the girls have since grown into young women with careers and homes of their own. A few have gone on to obtain degrees in higher education; some are married and have families. These are true stories.

Lorie

The assembled team settled in around the large boardroom table.

The Exit Counselor, acting as coordinator, used a felt-tipped marker to note the names of those in attendance on a wall-mounted white board. Heading the list was the word "Mom."

As the mother introduced herself to those in attendance and related the agony of the past year and a half, the other people seated around the table asked questions and made notes.

Through their probing, details of Lorie's life—before she hit the streets—became clearer. Although her stepfather had sexually abused the young girl, her mother had refused to listen to these allegations, fearing that Lorie had concocted the stories to drive a wedge between Lorie's mother and her new husband.

Finally, Lorie had enough and headed to the streets. It was this desperate act that motivated the mother to make changes in her life and to accept the reality that her new husband—Lorie's stepfather—had not only abused Lorie, but also sexually abused a younger sister.

The police officer sketched a map of locations where they had spotted Lorie over the past two weeks and provided a list of her known associates. The team lawyer related several minor criminal charges laid against Lorie and advised the group of various legal options. A child psychologist, familiar with such cases, outlined a number of characteristics and attitudes that the child would likely have developed during the last year and a half on the street. Fear, uncertainty, confusion, guilt—these were but a few of the symptoms that Lorie would probably be displaying.

The family doctor, a general practitioner, made a brief appearance to let the team know that all Lorie's medical files were now in her office and that there would be no delay in accessing the necessary medical treatment.

The psychologist and physician excused themselves from the meeting and the remaining members of the team began their work. The team tossed around ideas, put forward strategies and modified them, and after three hours they agreed on a course of action.

On Friday night, Lorie was working her usual corner. A street outreach van pulled to the curb and chatted with the young prostitute. Lorie knew the Outreach workers from previous contacts and readily agreed to coffee and a short break away from the street.

The restaurant was quiet as the group slid into their usual booth. Jeanette, a thirty-something woman, joined the gathering and the workers introduced her. Trusting the Outreach workers, Lorie readily accepted the woman into the circle.

During the next two weeks, the coffee break became a regular occurrence in Lorie's routine. It seemed that at each meeting a new participant joined the group. First a lawyer who was a friend of the outreach workers, dropped in for a moment. During the course of the conversation, he offered to help Lorie in any way he could. Another night, a therapist visited—and finally a police officer. At each meeting, the group validated a new visitor's legitimacy, and because each one had been vouched for by Outreach, she accepted their presence.

Her comfort level grew with each meeting. In the warmth and security of the coffee shop, her story unfolded. Lorie also confirmed their belief that she missed her mom and wanted to reconnect. The team had set the stage.

At their next gathering, Jeanette, the woman who had been the first to join the group, casually dropped a significant bit of information into the conversation—Lorie's mother had contacted her that morning. Within the tranquillity of the group, Lorie accepted the news with feigned indifference. Her "so-what?" attitude, anticipated by the other members at the table, nonetheless signalled that a bond still existed in Lorie's mind between mother and daughter. It was a bond they intended to use.

Passing over a cell phone, Jeanette suggested Lorie give her mom a call, "Just to let her know you're alive." Lorie took the phone and dialed.

The phone answered on the second ring. "Hi Mom, it's me." First, a look of disbelief came over Lorie's face, followed shortly by tears and the words "Mom...it's okay...really...it's okay!" For the next half minute Lorie repeated only those words. Finally, she lowered the phone from her ear and stared at it. "She wouldn't talk. She just cried. Then she hung up!"

Weeks earlier, the team mapped out their plan to get her back from the clutches of the street and reunite her with her mother. They had coached the mother, and unknown to Lorie, they orchestrated this first contact, as well as her mom's response.

The following evening, Lorie sat with the regular group; she turned and looked through the window. There, looking back at her was her mother. Struggling to get out of the booth, she grabbed one of the Outreach workers and scrambled for the door. By the time she emerged from the café, her mother was half a block away, sliding behind the wheel of her car. Lorie was too late to catch her. She tucked herself into the arms of the Outreach worker and sobbed. She couldn't understand why her mother was running away from her—it was so unlike her mom! In the months previous to the "coffee meets," Lorie's mother had been very aggressive. She demanded that her child change her ways and threatened to have her arrested. Now she was passive, withdrawing from confrontation, not initiating communication. In effect, she was making Lorie come to her.

Acting as a bridge between Lorie and her mother, Jeanette, who was filling the role of Exit Counselor, arranged to have Mom drop in on one of the regular coffee gatherings.

The brief meeting was cordial but strained—but it was a beginning. When Lorie learned that her mother had barred the stepfather from the home and pressed criminal charges against him, her reconnection with her mother seemed only a matter of time.

The coffee meetings evolved into day long outings for Lorie and her mother. The day meetings expanded to become weekends at home. The lawyer kept his promise to advocate for a period of probation on Lorie's charges, and the therapist made room in her schedule for twice-weekly sessions with the young girl.

Using their contacts in the community, the outreach workers registered Lorie in an "alternative" school and within eight months she regained her educational status and re-entered the regular school system.

Still, the whole process of recovery has been a struggle, and the struggle has not been without its setbacks. Lorie's self-imposed guilt and shame for her actions often threatened to overwhelm her. From time to time Lorie remembered some of the good times she had on the street and the friends she'd left behind after she returned home. It was during these periods that the team would get back together and help her survive these difficult moments.

It's now been almost two years since the team first assembled in that boardroom. Lorie is now seventeen years old. She dates. She plays basketball on the school team. She worries about her complexion. She argues with her Mom. She just got her navel pierced. She smokes. She can't decide what to do after graduation. She's a normal teenager.

Jennifer

The call came at 1:00 A.M. Both parents had long been asleep, even though Jennifer was several hours late for her curfew. It had been this way for several months and both her mom and dad had grown weary of trying to enforce a curfew that just didn't seem to have any hope of being honored.

At the other end of the line, the Desk Sergeant at Police Headquarters didn't mince words. "Your daughter was arrested for prostitution. You'll have to come down to City Cells and attend the hearing to determine release conditions."

The conversation in the car during the twenty minute drive to the station was one of stunned disbelief. "No.... The officer had obviously made a mistake.... Our daughter a prostitute?... How had this happened?... Did it happen?... Why?... Did we make some horrible mistake in raising her?... Is she on drugs?... Where is her boyfriend?"

"*That* must be it—her boyfriend.... I never trusted him.... But Jennifer was so in love with the guy we let it go. We thought it would pass like her other teenage crushes."

They hadn't yet fully grasped the idea of their daughter being a prostitute. By the time they found a place to park, however, they made up their minds to spare no effort or expense in reclaiming their child.

The door buzzed and they entered the chrome and leatherette waiting room of the booking office. They didn't have to wait very long before a bearded man walked over to them. His clothes were scruffy and dirty; his hair tied back in a ponytail. Reaching into his pocket, he pulled out a badge and introduced himself as an undercover vice officer.

Quickly sketching the details of the case for the stunned parents, he walked them back through a short hallway separating the Juvenile Cells from the adult area. The officer opened the door to a small room and ushered them inside. "I'll be back with Jennifer in a moment," he said quietly, closing the door behind him.

Yells and curses preceded Jennifer's arrival. Her parents had never heard their child utter such profanity, even when she was in one of her foulest moods. They sat, shocked into silence.

The door opened to reveal a Jennifer they'd never seen before. She stood before them in a short miniskirt, push-up bra and bare midriff. She was barefoot. The police had obviously taken her shoes. She struggled against the grip of the vice officer, hurling four letter words into his face. She saw her parents, whirled to face them, and sneered, "So now you know—your good little girl is a *ho!*"

The words tore through their hearts. They no longer doubted their beautiful daughter's involvement in something so horrible and demeaning that even hearing the word was painful.

The old cop leaned against the doorway with arms folded, a resigned look on his passive face. Even though he'd witnessed similar scenes many times before, he never got used to the fact that a child's outrageous actions came as such a surprise to parents. He knew that Jennifer's run to the street hadn't taken place over one or two days—this had been building for quite a while. The parents had chosen to ignore the warning signs and now there was a mountain of difficulties to overcome to rescue their child.

The reunion was brief. Jennifer stood obstinately in front of her parents, hands on her hips, jaw thrust defiantly forward. Accusations of not caring what happened to her mixed with tears and apologies for putting her parents in this situation. Obviously she felt conflicted: confused, embarrassed, and angry, she didn't know where to direct her outbursts. The officer returned Jennifer to her cell.

The next two hours were painful for the parents, yet necessary in their education of what child prostitution is all about. Briefed about the recruiting methods used by predatory pimps, they became aware of the controls pimps impose on the young and naïve. They learned that the recovery process was not going to be easy and that, before it began, the parents had to commit to both the process and the cost.

The vice officer outlined those costs in terms of time, emotion, energy, personal commitment and money. This was going to be a contest—a battle—between the parents and the pimp who had taken Jennifer from them. Without hesitation, both parents vowed to get their daughter back.

The officer recommended that Jennifer remain in jail for the night. Although it went against their protective instincts to take Jennifer home, they listened to his detailed rationale and agreed to leave her in custody.

Then the officer shared his knowledge about Caleb—Jennifer's pimp. At twenty-six, Caleb had a history of recruiting girls in their early teens by romancing them for a period of time and then putting them out on the street as prostitutes. The officer's information revealed that Jennifer was the eighth adolescent turned out by Caleb. He'd never stood trial for his crimes because the police were never able to convince a girl to "sign on him."

Given Jennifer's continued infatuation with Caleb, the parents and the officer decided that a legal process would be in Jennifer's best interests. It was a plan of action that wasn't without risk, for as the officer counseled, Jennifer would probably become less contrite and even further enraged with her parents. After much discussion, this course of action seemed to be the only rational alternative.

When court convened the next morning, the undercover officer laid criminal charges against Jennifer for offering sexual services for money. A lawyer, retained by the parents, asked for a period of secure treatment for the youngster. After learning that she was only fourteen, that her behavior was out of control, and that she presented a significant danger to herself, the judge agreed.

For the next thirty days, Jennifer found herself confined to a treatment facility. As predicted, she was furious with her parents for "doing this to her." For the first ten days, she refused to have any contact with them, and when they came to visit, she wouldn't leave her room. The only outsider allowed contact with her was an outreach worker who had befriended Jennifer while she was on the street. This worker kept the parents informed about their daughter's progress.

Daily one-on-one sessions with the Center's psychiatrist helped Jennifer through this difficult time. Through these encounters she came to grips with what had transpired on the street and how Caleb had used her. The Center's imposed structure helped her stabilize her life. Getting out of bed at 7:00 A.M., showing up for meals at fixed times, and structuring her day according to organized activities, were stabilizing factors in Jennifer's life—a life that had been without form or shape for the period of time she was with Caleb.

After thirty days, Jennifer came home. Still angry and bitter, she railed against the new situation in the home and the conditions of her probation. Her mother took a leave-of-absence from her work and stayed home with Jennifer. Family routines adjusted to accommodate the new reality of restructured home dynamics. Jennifer continued with weekly therapy, and the court assigned her to community service working with a street agency dealing with child prostitution. A tutor aided in restoring Jennifer's education to her peer's level, and the whole family attended weekly group sessions at a parent support network.

The home telephone, now equipped with a device to record all incoming phone numbers, also had a long-distance call block put on it. A new rule required anyone visiting Jennifer to come inside and meet with either her mother or father. The street agency continued their contact with the youngster, visiting her home at least once a week. Through them, Jennifer established a safe bridge between the street world and the straight world.

Three months after Jennifer's return home, she once again headed back to her street corner. This time, the police immediately picked her up for breaching probation and the judge imposed even more stringent guidelines. He provided, however, a window of opportunity for her to open. He decreed that if Jennifer abided by the imposed conditions and completed her community hours within the next three months, he would amend the probation order to allow her a later curfew.

Gradually Jennifer settled down into the routine of this new existence. She agreed to enroll in an outdoor activity program, and the adrenaline rush of whitewater rafting, bungee jumping and mountain climbing served her well in replacing the thrills and excitement of street life. Life at home became less "boring."

The most noticeable breakthrough happened when she volunteered to continue helping with the Street Agency—even though she'd fulfilled her community hours.

Is she cured? No. It will be years before the wounds of child prostitution begin to heal. She's making the effort though, and day by day, life is becoming what it should be for Jennifer and her family.

Sharon

The rough pavement felt strange to her feet. She looked down past her stained T-shirt and scruffy jeans to her bare toes. This was the ultimate humiliation: she had been "lowered" by her pimp. Only this morning she had been a classy "hi-track" girl, wearing thigh-high leather boots and the best clothing. Now what was she? A "low-track" bitch who had been thoroughly "dissed" and put out as a 24−7 (forced to work 24 hours a day, 7 days a week).

Sharon ran away from an abusive home when she was twelve years old. Apprehended by Children's Aid, she became a permanent ward of the state by the time she was fifteen. A chance meeting with a pimp at an after-hours club was all it took for her to reject society and head out for a life as a street prostitute.

For four long years, she moved from city to city. Her "men" maintained many connections across the country. When the police initiated a series of raids and crackdowns in one city, Sharon would simply be moved to another.

A number of attempts to rescue her from the clutches of her pimp had failed. While well-meaning, most of the undertakings were done by do-gooders—"social tourists" as they are called on the street. Church groups, social workers doing required practicums, and various outreach programs had all promised help, yet when the time came, each one fell far short of being able to deliver on their pledge.

Sharon became bitter and cynical. She didn't trust "the system" in any guise. Still, she had to admit, although she didn't like the police, she learned over the years that at least *they* kept their promises: if she was on the street, they arrested her and put her in jail overnight. It wasn't pleasant, but at least they were predictable.

Sharon lost count of the number of times she was sold or traded from one pimp to another over the last four years. This most recent pimp, however, was the most violent of them all. When she first joined his stable, she thought that he might be an improvement over her previous pimps because this one promised to make her his senior prostitute or "main." With that designation, she expected not to have to work as many hours. She would just help her man collect the nightly take or "trap" from the other girls in his stable.

Three weeks after being passed along to the new pimp, Sharon developed a cyst on the inside of her calf. It soon festered, developing into a very serious medical condition. She realized she needed urgent treatment at the nearby walk-in clinic, and she told her man that she couldn't go out on the street.

No sooner had the words left her lips than she realized she'd said the wrong thing. The pimp swung around and viciously hit her in the stomach with his fist. When she collapsed on the floor, he kicked her in the back several times. Then, grabbing her hair, he yanked her to her feet.

"Think you're too good to be a working ho do you? Think that just 'cause I made you my main, you can take a day off whenever you *feel* like it? You've had an attitude ever since I got you. Startin' today—*that's* gonna change."

Roughly shoving her along in front of him, he pushed her into the bedroom. Grabbing some of her dirty clothes from the floor, he held them in front of her face.

"Wear these!" he commanded.

Sobbing, she donned the old jeans and T-shirt. She slipped into four-inch heels, but he threw her to the floor and snatched them from her feet.

"You're worked flat now—no shoes at all," he screamed at her.

For Sharon this was the ultimate humiliation. Her pimp was 'dissing her and putting her out on the street with no shoes. She never before felt so embarrassed.

When her pimp informed her that she was now 24–7 and being put on the low-track with the injection addicts, her shame was complete.

On the street, as she stood looking down at her exposed feet, the realization finally hit her—if she was going to break free from the life, it was up to her.

Glancing up from her feet, she watched two cars approach from either end of the block. The one travelling on her side of the road was obviously a john, the other a marked patrol car. She made a decision.

Crossing the street, Sharon reached for the rear door handle of the police car.

"Take me to Vice. I have a story to tell." With those words she left the game.

As fortune would have it, the on-duty vice detective was having coffee with the executive director of a recovery home for street prostitutes. Answering his cell phone, he responded immediately. Instructing the uniformed officers to take Sharon to the vice office, he turned to the director and excused himself. Timing was critical.

Videotaping the session as well as taking notes, the detective recorded Sharon's statement over a five hour period. Names, dates, places, amounts, people and activities: all went into the record of Sharon's four year stint in prostitution. She not only signed on her most recent pimp, but three others who had previously owned her.

Later that night, the detective introduced Sharon to the director who had been having coffee with him earlier. She hugged Sharon and told her she would be welcome in the Center for as long as she needed to stay. That was all the young girl needed to hear. She was ready.

The detective arranged for a lawyer to meet with Sharon and to craft a restraining order against her pimp. The document, sworn before a Senior Judge, prevented the pimp from having contact with Sharon in any way. The judge forbade him to phone, write, visit—or have someone do it for him—and if he breached these orders, he would be arrested and placed in jail.

A volunteer Victim Assistance Counselor from the Police Department met with Sharon and detailed the legal proceedings that she was facing. It was going to be an ordeal. The counselor painstakingly coached Sharon in the skills she would need in giving testimony at various trials. She told her how to handle aggressive cross-examination and how to deal with courtroom pressures. In addition, she prepared Sharon for the two or three year process that lay in front of her before she could put closure on all the legal wrangling.

Sharon has now been in the Center for eighteen months. Coaching and courage guided her through a myriad of legal battles. Enrolled in a correspondence course, she's preparing to enter a community college. Already her determination is evident in the results of her first set of examinations—she's excelling.

Someday she hopes to become a social worker.

Sharon wants to change the system.

Maria

His brown hair had grown gray over the past few months; deep worry lines etched his face. He couldn't understand what had happened. His beloved daughter Maria had fallen in love with a man nine years her senior, and had moved in with him.

He'd hired a local private investigator to track down his daughter, and he now had the address where she lived. He jammed the filmy piece of paper into his vest pocket as he stood in front of the door, quietly shaking with anger and frustration.

Moments before, he had knocked on the door and met the twenty-five year old man with whom his daughter was living. Predictably, the meeting between these two strangers hadn't gone well.

At first, the man wouldn't allow the father into the apartment, however, one mention of the word "police" and the fellow relented and allowed him in.

Maria had just gotten out of bed, and when she saw her father, she ran forward and threw her arms around him. Happy to see him, she blithely assumed that now her father had met her boyfriend, he shared her feelings. She felt stunned when her agitated father told her to pack her things and come with him.

"But I love him! I want to be here with him," she protested. "Why can't you just accept that?"

When her father again demanded she accompany him, she retreated into the living room and put her arms around her boyfriend. Defiantly she shouted at her father, "I'm staying—and there's nothing you can do about it. I'm sixteen and I can make up my own mind how to live my life."

For another five minutes the father argued fruitlessly with his daughter. He cajoled her, told her he and her mother loved her, and then, appealing to her rational side he played out his last card and revealed all the information obtained by the private investigator. Her boyfriend was a pimp. She flatly refused to believe him.

"Yes," she acknowledged. She knew that girls gave him money. Her boyfriend had explained it all to her, saying that the girls "owed him" for various things, such as transportation, food and the like. Any doubts she had evaporated long ago. Ignoring her father's evidence, she chose not to believe that her boyfriend was anything other than what he seemed to be—a charming man, a loving partner, and a generous friend.

Still arguing with his daughter, the father was ushered out of the apartment by the smirking boyfriend. Maria stood in the living room with her arms crossed in front of her body, shaking her head. Her father's inclination was to smash his fist into the face of the man standing between them, but he remembered the investigator's warnings. Fearing this kind of reaction, he had cautioned the father not to go to their address. The investigator reasoned that it would do his daughter no good if he landed in jail. It took all the father's self-control to back out of the room. The door slammed in his face.

Downstairs in the lobby, he put his arms around his wife and wept. This was a new low point in his life—would they ever see their daughter again? He knew he needed help.

The private investigator had given him a list of service agencies who specialized in dealing with young prostitutes. At this point, he had nothing to lose; he reached for the phone.

A team quickly assembled. This situation was different from most because both parents felt involved, and there was obviously a deep love between the father and daughter—although the presence of the pimp temporarily blinded the daughter's affection. On that basis the team made plans.

The police officer provided the team with information about Maria's pimp. From the Caribbean, he had been in the country for about a year, and fancied himself as quite an athlete, participating in sports such as basketball, karate and weightlifting.

Through interviews with the parents, the team discovered that Maria herself was an accomplished athlete. Her chosen sport, however, was skiing. Her father told the group about Maria's advanced abilities—she'd achieved a high-expert ranking as a downhill skier. He further revealed that both he and Maria enjoyed running the double black-diamond runs in the mountains, and it was at those times that they were closest.

The team planned the operation. It was risky. There was a chance that, in the contest to come, the father would be the loser. It was a risk worth taking, however, for they could see no other alternative.

A member of the team sent a message to Maria. This message contained the information that her dad wanted to make amends. The story was that he'd rented a chalet at one of the most sought-after ski resorts in the Canadian Rockies, and he was inviting both Maria and her boyfriend to come and spend a weekend with family.

Maria was ecstatic. Perhaps her family was coming around to accept her new situation! She loved skiing. This was one resort where she'd always badgered her dad to take her. "It's the ultimate!", she enthused to her boyfriend. "And, it has four double expert runs, including one called *The Cliff*, with an 37° slope." What a great dad her father was—inviting both of them. She dashed for the bedroom to pack. "You'll just love it!", she shouted over her shoulder.

The invitation infuriated the pimp. Being from the tropics, he'd never learned to ski. He had no idea what an 37° slope was. In fact, up until a year ago, he'd never seen snow other than in pictures! He felt boxed in.

If he forbade Maria to go, she would be angry and would side with her father against him.

If he let her go by herself, the father would have Maria all to himself, and away from the influence of the pimp. Who knew what could happen?

The only alternative was to graciously accept the invitation and to keep Maria in his sights at all times.

The weekend arrived and, while they took separate flights, both Maria and her boyfriend joined Maria's parents at the resort within minutes of each other.

Maria ran to her dad and threw her arms around him. She now had two heroes—her boyfriend and her father! This weekend was going to be great!

The first hint that things weren't going to unfold as smoothly as she hoped, was when Maria went with her boyfriend to the rental shop. He didn't know anything! For the first time, she was in control. She instructed the technician on the kind of skis he needed, the length of poles and the type of bindings and boots. Mom and Dad had brought her own skis from home.

There was still enough light to make several runs down the mountain, and Maria was eager to show her boyfriend her skills.

They took the double chair lift to make the first run. It was a disaster. Getting off the lift, the pimp got his skis tangled and went nose first into the snow. All his touted athletic ability evaporated.

Angrily he got back on his feet and pushed off down the slope.

Later, Mom and Dad wished they'd brought their camcorder. The pimp was a sight. Falling, then getting back up, he just fell again. He became angry. Maria demonstrated great patience in trying to instruct her boyfriend on the basics of the "snowplow" to gently coax him down the run, but she couldn't help laughing at his efforts. That infuriated him even more.

She suggested he try the bunny slope—"Just to get used to the skis." He refused.

By the end of the afternoon, it was apparent that even Maria had given up hope that he'd learn enough to keep up with her on even the novice slopes. *The Cliff* beckoned to her—she'd anticipated it for so many years.

For the final run of the day, Maria asked her father to go with her to the famous double black-diamond run. She could barely conceal her excitement as they rode the summit chair.

Laughing and challenging each other on the way down, they raced to the bottom of the run. Her father slipped the lift operator a $20 bill and they were able to catch one more run before the chair lift closed for the day.

When the jubilant skiers returned to the lodge, they discovered that Maria's boyfriend had taken a cab back into town. He left a message at the reception desk demanding Maria catch the next flight back to the city and join him. His childish message denounced skiing as "a stupid waste of time" and reproached her for making him look like a fool in front of her parents.

Disgusted, Maria threw the note in the wastebasket.

It was a risk but, in the end, the team's plan worked. Dad won. Maria won. The family is in therapy, but they are together.

10

"What Can I Do?"

My grandpa said he loved me, and then he raped me.
My mom said she loved me, and then beat me with a broom handle.
My pimp said he loved me, and then turned me out as a prostitute.
The johns said they loved me,
then made me have sex with them when I was thirteen.
What do you mean when you tell me you want to give me love?

IN all cultures, the objectification of children as commodities in a sex-for-sale business is the ultimate betrayal of trust—the betrayal of children by adults. It is not just the betrayal of a female by a male, although the pimps and users are almost exclusively male. It is not just a betrayal of a little girl by a father figure, although this is often the case. It is not just the betrayal of children by our society, although we are the ones who should be protecting our youth. Who do we condemn for this treachery?

We can, and should, condemn the pimps. They entice and coerce young children into the degrading and violent world of prostitution. They rob these children of their self-esteem, their sense of self-worth, their natural growth, and their very childhood. When they transform a girl into a product—a saleable, disposable commodity—they destroy her fundamental personhood and deny her rights as a human being. The pimp inflicts permanent damage that results in lifelong scars or even the death of a child.

We must condemn the customers, who with a few dollars, satisfy their perversion by purchasing children and subjecting them to statutory rape. Their collective appetites nourish the marketplace in a downward spiral of increasingly deviant behavior. It is their money that fuels the fire of violence and destruction of these little ones. We cannot and should not call these people "johns." They are pedophiles.

We should also condemn legislators and law makers. Reluctance or apathy prevents them from using their power to enact legislation that would elevate the crime of sexually exploiting children and make it worthy of extensive prison terms. Our courts sentence bank robbers—who only steal our money—to lengthy periods of incarceration, but to those who steal our children, it extends an average of half as much time.

Some social service agencies—especially the ones who view the young prostitutes as having "chosen an alternative lifestyle," and do not help the girls escape—cannot themselves escape our criticism, if not our condemnation. Those charged with the responsibility of protecting our youth are obligated to re-educate their profession, to change their perspectives about child prostitutes and to understand the girls as victims.

But before we can target anyone for blame or condemnation, we must first shoulder the blame and condemnation ourselves. We are the ones who allow child prostitution to continue and to flourish, and only we can change that. What can we do?

Our society needs to understand child prostitution, recognize its victims, and take responsibility for launching the war to eradicate it from our culture and from the world. We need to keep in mind the model of the World Health Organization as we take our battle to global arenas. We need to reclaim the power of our common decency.

We have the knowledge base to combat the pimps. We have the power to publicly expose those who buy the services of these children. We can claim the power of the ballot to elect and support legislators in changing the laws. We can demand officers of the courts pursue and mete out stiffer sentences for sexual crimes against children. We have the power to demand changes to our social service programs and especially to provide education for those who work with these young girls. The tasks in this war seem daunting, but we have no choice but to engage the enemy.

Children in the Game and *The Butterfly Collectors* use true stories to educate people about child prostitution. In many oral societies, telling stories is a way of telling about life. "Tell the life like a story," is more than a cultural technique for explaining how a society functions, it serves to form perceptions and to suggest solutions. Yet, solutions are sometimes transparent, seemingly beyond our grasp. When I finish telling the stories about some of the children in "the life"—whether it's before a huge audience, or a small group of people, or a single individual—the final question is always the same: "What can I do?" Marked by a sense of helplessness, the inquiry is nonetheless genuine and urgent.

The outlook for the future is not all bleak. There *are* answers to the question, "What can I do?" There are ways you can participate in the war. By raising awareness of the problems surrounding child prostitution, becoming knowledgeable in exit techniques, changing our attitudes towards the girls, and taking appropriate action, we can influence three important outcomes:

1. the prevention of children being recruited as prostitutes,
2. the intervention in control systems used by pimps in order to facilitate the recovery of child prostitutes and,
3. the recovery of these young girls as they reconnect with their parents, relatives, or caring adults.

The overriding conclusion of *Children in the Game* is that no matter how damaged, these young girls are recoverable and valuable. There is hope for them because we have a team approach with procedures that can and do work to remove a child from prostitution and then to re-integrate her into a world with a future.

Little girls should not have to live in fear of the adults charged with the task of protecting them.

We have often heard that our children are *our* future.

For these children—we are *their* future.

Glossary of
"Street Talk"

BELIEVING the best defense is a good offense, my goal has been to educate readers of *Children in the Game* by describing the sub-culture of prostitution. A critical factor of understanding "the life" is being familiar with its unique vocabulary which carries the linguistic baggage of logic, values, social structures, and beliefs. This glossary lists frequently used street terms. Words in *italics* are cross-references to other entries.

action – The degree of business activity e.g. "Lots of action going on".

active – A pimp who is busy recruiting new girls and doing business.

around the world – Oral sex and various forms of intercourse. Generally this is the "top" service provided and is the most expensive.

animal trainer – A person—either prostitute or customer—who engages in bestiality.

attitude – Refers to a way of thinking and behaving that is generally negative, hence in the phrase "bad attitude," the word "bad" is redundant. Other modifiers may be used. For example when describing a person's "big shot attitude", the speaker means the subject is always "bitchy" or complaining about things or events with contempt.

baby mom – Refers to a prostitute who is the birth mother of a pimp's baby. Generally given a higher place in the "family" than other women. Often privy to private conversations between the pimp and other players.

baby stroll, - track – An area of the city where child prostitutes are found.

bad date – A customer who refuses to pay or abuses the prostitute. Can range from a simple refusal to pay, to a forced rape.

bad date sheet – A written record that circulates in every city. It contains reports of bad dates, describes the incidents, and frequently provides a description of the person, the vehicle, and the license plate number of the offender.

beats – A serious assault on a prostitute or other street person. May be laid on by the pimp, however is very often orchestrated by the pimp but then carried out by other prostitutes.

being alive – Active pimp—in the "life." Generally a term referring to a mid-level pimp with three to eight prostitutes under his control. Only a pimp who is actively marketing his prostitutes is considered "live."

bill – A hundred dollars. See *three-o'clock* which is the metaphor for three bills or $300.

bitch – A term used to refer to women in general.

blanked – To not make money or have any customers during the time of work. May also be reference to a time frame when business is poor, e.g., "Blanked until just after midnight."

blow – Street term for cocaine. (See also *snow*).

blow / blow job – Act of oral sex or fellatio, to ejaculation.

break – The occasion when money is collected by the prostitute for sexual services, e.g., "Broke six times, and still didn't meet my quota."

bump / bumping – To coerce or convince another pimp's prostitute to work for you. Will sometimes also be used erroneously to refer to the recruiting of a new prostitute.

charge – A monetary sum to be paid by the prostitute to her pimp for some particular action. Mostly used as a method of control to keep the prostitute in perpetual debt to the pimp. (See also *street charge, leaving fee, choosing fee*).

chase off – The act of protecting one's territory. A prostitute may chase off another girl from her territory on the stroll.

cheap – A customer who tries to undercut the prostitute's stated price or to obtain sexual services for less than the going rates. (See also *useless date*).

choose / choosing up – When a prostitute chooses a new or different pimp. This occurs when a pimp has lost influence as a serious player, when he is jailed, or when he releases her on a *charge*.

choosing fee – A monetary sum levied on a prostitute who chooses a new or different pimp. This money must be made by her and given to the new pimp. The old pimp will receive a *leaving fee*.

choosy suzy – A prostitute who moves from one pimp to another pimp at very regular intervals.

cop check – Techniques used by prostitutes to determine if a potential customer is an undercover police officer. A technique frequently employed by a prostitute is to request her date to simultaneously touch her breasts or genitals as she touches his.

couch surfing – Moving from one friend's house to another on a regular basis, sometimes sleeping on a different couch every night of the week. A survival tactic.

crack head – Refers to a prostitute who is addicted to crack cocaine and charges very low rates.

crack lay – Sexual intercourse paid for with an amount of crack cocaine instead of money.

cutters – Refers to self-inflicted slashing with a knife to arms and torso.

date – A person who obtains the services of a prostitute.

dinner – Slang term for sexual intercourse. Often used to try and outwit the police or in the belief that it will serve as a defense in court.

'dis or dissing – A term used to indicate that a prostitute is not showing respect to her pimp. A serious offense and will guarantee a beating.

dogging – The action taken by a pimp to condition his prostitute to accept some very unpleasant activities. The word comes from the methods used to train a dog. A beating followed by a shower of affection, treats and special considerations, then another beating. The prostitute becomes disoriented, not knowing right from wrong. She feels everything is her fault, and will do just about anything to receive the praise and love from the pimp.

double – Two prostitutes on a date with two johns, or two prostitutes with a single customer.

drag – The area where prostitutes walk the street and solicit business. (See also *stroll, track*). May also refer to the style of clothing worn by a male person dressed in female clothing.

dress code – An informal agreement between the prostitutes as to how they will dress in order to keep the competition fair. Often the police understand this code and will remind the girls of it, in order to prevent violence on the strolls. For example, a prostitute will not wear excessively expensive clothes if the area is a lower class stroll. The reason is an ironic sense of fair and unfair competition.

drinks – Slang term for fellatio. Often used to try and outwit the police, or in the belief that it will serve as a defense in court.

drinks and dinner – A slang term for fellatio to erection then intercourse. Refers to a *half and half*, and used to try and outwit the police.

drug track / druggie stroll / drunky stroll – An area of the city where prostitutes who are drug or alcohol dependent work for low rates in order to pay for their next high.

fag hag – A derogatory term applied to a woman who associates with male prostitutes. Will occasionally act as a pimp for a male prostitute.

fag stroll – An area of the city where male prostitutes work; where males come to pick up other males for sexual services.

first break – The first trick the prostitute pulls in the evening for which she receives money.

flashing / flash rolls – The action of a pimp who is showing off his clothes, car, jewelry etc. to impress a prospective prostitute or other pimp.

game or "the game" – The life of a pimp and his prostitutes. It is viewed as an exciting game between players in *the life*. Taking women from each other, outwitting the police and living dangerously.

gay-for-pay – A prostitute who is not a true homosexual, but will engage in homosexual acts for pay.

Greek – Anal intercourse.

half and half – Fellatio and intercourse.

hand job – Masturbation of the customer, by the prostitute, to ejaculation.

high-end / high-track – Refers to both prostitutes who have higher fees and to the area of the city in which they are found. They are generally better dressed—often "glamorously" outfitted in fine clothes and impeccable makeup. Characteristically, high-track prostitutes are highly organized under the tight control of a pimp with considerable power. The high-track is very territorial. The opposite of *low-track*.

hoe / ho – Female prostitute.

jacked up – An action taken, usually by other prostitutes, to bring another prostitute into line. Often for things like undercutting prices, working without a pimp, or other street rule violations. For example, the other prostitutes would assault a new girl working without a pimp, as she may be taking their customers. This would be referred to as "jacking her up."

john – Male customer.

juice – A pimp who is viewed as courageous in dealing with other pimps, the police or tough prostitutes. He would be seen as having "the juice to do it."

lay – Sexual intercourse. A standard service provided by prostitutes. (See also *straight lay*).

leaving fee – An amount levied against the prostitute by the pimp in order for her to get out of the life of prostitution. Generally is an amount she will never be able to pay off, and so becomes a debt that is never erased. (See also *charges*).

life or "the life" – Being involved in pimping or prostitution in general (See also *the game*).

live – Refers to a pimp who is active in the game of prostitution.

live club – A bar where pimps hang out and where they may take their girls in the off hours. Often the location where *choosing* takes place, or where territory is established or negotiated.

look or the look – Refers to a prostitute's technique of making direct eye-contact that invites conversation with a potential customer.

low-track – Refers to both prostitutes who have lower fees and to the area of the city in which they are found. Generally they are not well dressed. The opposite of *high-track*.

mack or mack daddy – A well-established pimp who is often involved in the *high-end* trade with Escort Agencies or Massage Parlors where he works his girls. He very often has a home in the suburbs and his neighbors are not aware of his occupation.

main – The most influential woman in a pimp's group of prostitutes. Frequently the one he lives with. Often she does his collections, enforces his rules, sets prices, etc. Sometimes referred to as the pimp's *wifey*.

man – Pimp, as in "My Man" or "Her Man."

minder – A term used by the police to refer to someone who looks after the girls. Sometimes this is an older girl or a woman who is given the responsibility by a pimp or gang to keep all the young prostitutes together and in line. She sometimes functions as a "babysitter."

partner – A prostitute who teams up with another prostitute to look after each other while working. They will note license numbers of cars, keep track of each other's time away from the street and, in general, serve as a safety factor.

pass-around – Refers to a prostitute who works "inside." A practice common in eastern North America, the pimp places the prostitute in one part of a room and sells her services to men who come to the site. In the vernacular, he "sells her right off the counter."

pimp stick – A coat hanger that is unraveled, doubled over, and used to whip a prostitute for perceived infractions or for showing a lack of respect for her man. Sometimes it will be heated on a stove to increase the degree of pain.

player – A person involved in prostitution. Generally refers to a pimp, however prostitutes also view themselves as "players in the game."

player's ball – A social event in which pimps will take their *mains* and mingle with other players. They will go to great lengths to hide these events from the police.

popcorn pimp – A small time pimp who recruits young girls and runs them only until they are taken over by one of the more powerful pimps. A derogatory term referring to someone who has no influence or respect.

punked – The word used when a pimp has lost influence on the street. He has been made ineffective through the actions of the police, another pimp, or a prostitute.

quota – A specified amount of money that the prostitute must earn for the pimp before she can quit for the night.

recruiter – Refers to a person who selects potential prostitutes, breaks them in, then turns them over to the pimp.

regular – A customer who seeks out the same prostitute each time. Often they develop a pattern of contact, e.g., every Tuesday evening etc.

sign – An action whereby a prostitute signs a written statement on her pimp's activities for the police. Considered the ultimate act of disrespect towards a pimp.

sister – A friendly term of reference between girls working for the same pimp, or just between girls working or living on the street.

snow – Street term for cocaine; (See also *blow*).

soft – A slow night customer-wise.

spotter – A person who watches out for the police, bad dates or other undesirables. Often this action is used to condition a potential prostitute to life on the street. The person might be a girl who is not in the game, or a young man. The spotter's services are often exchanged for coffee, cigarettes, or even drugs.

square / straight – Any male or female not in "the game." A person not affiliated with prostitution.

square bitch – A female friend who is not a prostitute.

square boyfriend – Male friend who is not a pimp or in "the life."

squaring up – Leaving *the life*—leaving prostitution.

stable – A group of prostitutes all controlled by the same pimp.

stash – Money a prostitute will hide from her pimp. Considered a serious breach of protocol. This usually results in the serious beating of the prostitute by the pimp.

straight lay – A normal act of vaginal intercourse.

street charge – An amount of money levied by a pimp on a prostitute. One pimp may levy this fee against another pimp's girl as well. It may be for showing disrespect, undercutting prices, or just for speaking to him and not choosing him. (See also *charges*).

stroll – An area of the city where prostitutes walk. (See also *drag* and *track*).

sugar fly – A slightly pejorative term for a pimp that describes his flamboyant appearance and actions. The sugar fly fits the popularized image of a pimp, thus he is almost a caricature of a pimp with overdone, vivid clothing and gestures.

super fly – An experienced pimp with considerable power who controls several prostitutes. This term is used almost exclusively in eastern North America.

three o'clock – A metaphor or code for three bills or $300. (See also *bills*).

track – An area of the city where prostitutes walk. (See also *stroll* and *drag*).

tranny – A male posing as a female prostitute. A derivative of "transvestite."

trap – The money a prostitute earns and turns over to the pimp.

trashing – The act of a prostitute dressing up in working clothes to go on the street.

trick – Can refer either to the customer or to the act itself. For example, "Here comes a trick," or "She turned four tricks before midnight."

trick pad – A location where there are a number of men and young girls are brought to them for sex. Very secretive and often focused on specific ethnic or socially-based customer groups. (See also *working indoors*).

turn out – A new prostitute just starting out. For example, "She was turned out in July."

twenty-four–seven / 24–7 – A term meaning a prostitute is expected to work twenty-four hours a day, seven days a week—or work until she drops in her tracks from exhaustion. Refers to a method of punishment or humiliation.

undo-able – A term meaning that a person is believed to be beyond authority, "un-catchable" in attempts to apprehend him or her by authorities.

useless date – A customer who tries to undercut the prostitute's stated price or to obtain sexual services for less than the going rates. (See also *cheap*).

water sport – Urination used as a sexual stimulation. Sometimes referred to as the "golden shower."

wife-in-law / wifey / wife – An assistant or second prostitute in the pimp's "family" or "stable." This second prostitute is subordinate to the main prostitute.

winky – Term of humorous derision used to describe a john who quickly reaches climax—who "comes within a wink-of-an-eye." Believed to be mostly attributable to a certain ethnic group.

working inside – A prostitute who works in a massage parlor or escort agency, or who services customers at any location other than on the street.

working outside – A prostitute who works on the street.

working indoors – A prostitute who works in a *trick pad*.

Yo-ho – Young prostitute generally under the age of eighteen.

Selected Bibliography

THERE is a bewildering array of books, articles from journals and magazines, videos, and web sites that deal with the subject of child prostitution. Listed below are some of the books I believe provide valuable information, perspectives and assistance, followed by a listing of videos that give valuable insights into child prostitution. All but two of the books are listed in the 1997–98 edition of *Books in Print*. Those by Tom MacDonnell and Catherine Roman are no longer listed as in print but may be available through your local library.

Books

Barry, Kathleen L. (1984). *Female Sexual Slavery*. New York, NY: New York University Press. 336p. ISBN #: 0-8147-1069-7.

In an in-depth, college level look, not only at prostitution, but at the larger subject of sexual slavery, this author writes from a feminist viewpoint and covers a wide range of exploitation. Scholarly in nature, it seeks to address the "why?" of the women involved in destructive relationships.

Campagna, Daniel S., and Proffenberger, Donald L. (1987). *The Sexual Trafficking in Children: An Investigation of the Child Sex Trade*. Westport, CT: Auburn House. 264p. ISBN #: 0-86569-155-X.

This study covers five years of research by the authors. They interviewed the children, the users, and the various agencies who try to help the children. It is a valuable resource for members of the criminal justice community, as well as for social workers and parents.

Davis, Nanette J. (ed.), (1993). *Prostitution: An International Handbook on Trends, Problems, and Policies*. Westport, CT: Greenwood Press. 424p. ISBN #: 0-313-25754-X.

This excellent book compiles the research on prostitution in sixteen countries, including Canada and the United States. The authors address the past, present and future of the issues surrounding prostitution. An excellent resource, the book contains many references and an extensive bibliography.

Grossfeld, Stan (1997). *Lost Futures: Our Forgotten Children*. New York, NY: Aperture Foundation Inc. ISBN #: 0-89381-696-5.

One of the very few books that uses the eye of a camera to show the world the plight of children. From Egypt to America, this photojournalist has set before us in stark reality, children who have been abandoned, neglected, brutalized and exploited.

Hoigard, Cecilie and Finstad, Liv (1992). *Backstreets: Prostitution, Money, & Love*. University Park, PA: Pennsylvania State University Press. 238p. ISBN #: 0-271-00878-4.

This book examines the issue of prostitution in Norway. Based on years of research, it is a unique recounting of the issue through stories related by prostitutes, pimps, customers, and the police. The authors allow the reader an insight into how these individuals see themselves and the world they inhabit.

Jessome, Phonse (1996). *Somebody's Daughter: Inside the Halifax-Toronto Pimping Ring*. Halifax, NS: Nimbus. ISBN #: 1-55-109-174-7.

The author takes us inside the lives of prostitutes and pimps who operate in the Halifax region. A thorough work of investigative reporting, the book goes to great lengths—sometimes a little too extreme—to hide the identity of the "players."

Johnson, Joan J. (1992). *Teen Prostitution*. Danbury, CT: Franklin Watts Inc. 112p. ISBN #: 0-531-11099-0.

This very complete analysis of teen prostitution in the United States examines the backgrounds and lives of those children caught up in street life, and describes a number of programs that are used in prevention and recovery of these youngsters. Liberally sprinkled with quotes and statistics, it is an authoritative work suitable for grades 9–12 and young adults.

Lau, Evelyn (1996). *Runaway: Diary of a Street Kid*. Toronto, ON: HarperCollins. ISBN #: 0-00-638625-3.

Literally the diary of a young prostitute during the years 1986 to 1988, the book chronicles her feelings, beliefs, and emotions as well as the action on the street. Recently the subject of a television special, the book tells the story in a straightforward, no holds barred fashion, that is powerful, yet tragic. After the first half of the book, much of the writing is repetitive.

MacDonnell, Tom (1987). *Never Let Go: The Tragedy of Kristy Mcfarlane*. MacMillan of Canada. ISBN #: 0-7715-9508-5.

This is the story of a girl caught up in prostitution at the age of fourteen, and of her mother, Sheila, who fought pimps, the lure of the street—and even the system—in an attempt to reclaim her child. Well-written, the book intended to have a happy ending, but concludes with the discovery of Kristy's body in 1987. Moving and sensitive, the pace of the book is fast and readable.

Roman, Catherine (1989). *Bang for a Buck*. Toronto, ON: Somerville House Publishing. 386p. ISBN #: 0-921051-27-1.

This book is set in the late 1960s and early 1970s in various cities in Canada. It is a first person account of a girl from a broken home who ended up becoming a prostitute. While lively and entertainingly written, it is somewhat dated because it relates to street life twenty-five years ago.

Usry, Becky (1995). *Sisterhood of the Night: A True Story*. Far Hills, NJ: New Horizon. 304p. ISBN #: 0-88282-134-2.

Usry is also the founder of New Life, a program designed to help prostitutes as they leave the streets and enter the straight world. This book is a narrative of the author's experiences as she works with girls on the streets, and some of the harrowing experiences she endured.

Videos

There are a number of video and film productions about children who have been victimized through prostitution. Many are voyeuristic in nature, and others treat the subject frivolously or exploitatively. The following is a short list of videos I have viewed and believe to be credible, informative and accurate.

The Butterfly Collectors

Available from:
Street Teams Society
210, 1505 – 17 Avenue S.W.
Calgary, Alberta, Canada T2T 0E2
Phone: (403) 228 • 3390

Stolen Lives: Children in the Sex Trade

Available from:
Still Water Pictures
Suite 411, 425 Carrall Street
Vancouver, British Columbia, Canada V6B 6E3
Phone: (604) 681 • 821928

A&E's Investigative Reports: The Child Sex Trade

Available from:
Kurtis Productions
400 West Erie Street
Chicago, Illinios, U.S.A. 60610
Phone: (312) 951 • 5700

Children of the Night

Available from:
Children of the Night
14530 Sylvan Street
Van Nuys, California, U.S.A. 91411
Phone: (818) 908 • 1468

Resources and Assistance

I regularly receive phone calls from all over North America. Calls from concerned social workers and justice department officials. Calls from researchers who are looking for more information on the subject of child sexual exploitation. Calls from other agencies on the lookout for missing children, and calls from worried parents who are searching for their daughters and do not know where to turn.

Over the years I compiled a list of agencies, organizations and individuals that have exceptional knowledge of the issue, and are willing to share that knowledge with others. As their addresses, phone numbers, and staff changed, I dutifully modified my card file and made them available to those who inquired. With the burgeoning of the child prostitution industry, a corresponding swell of new response agencies have been formed, and keeping all the information current became increasingly difficult.

The miracle of the World Wide Web has made it possible to acquire up-to-the-minute information about where to turn for help and information. Instead of listing hundreds of agencies and organizations—and running the risk of missing some that are both new and important—I have provided a short listing of information data centers that you can access for information and assistance.

At the end of this section, ample space has been left for you to record and build your own list of resources and support agencies.

Child Welfare League of America
http://www.cwla.org

The *Child Welfare League of America* has nearly 1,000 member agencies that serve children, youths, and families across the country. The homepage of the CWLA, this site links over one hundred agencies that have created web sites of their own, and is constantly being updated. From Alaska to Vermont, this listing is one of the largest resource sites on the web.

Clark Net
http://www.clarknet.com/erd/

This is a unique web site that provides access and listings to emergency services throughout the world. If a parent wishes to contact a police agency in any jurisdiction, this is the site to check first. Many of the listings are hot links to the police organizations themselves, providing even more information and direct phone numbers to the various local Missing Persons Units, Vice Squads, or Juvenile Task Forces.

National Center for Missing and Exploited Children
http://www.ncmec.org

As the United States resource center for child protection, the NCMEC spearheads national efforts to locate and recover missing children and raise public awareness about ways to prevent child abduction, molesting, and sexual exploitation. A private, non-profit organization established in 1984, NCMEC operates under a congressional mandate and works in conjunction with the U.S. Department of Justice's office of *Juvenile Justice and Delinquency Prevention*.

National Children's Coalition
http://www.child.net/citykids.htm

Operated by the *National Children's Coalition*, this web site is one of the most extensive on the net. Resources for children and teens in every major U.S. city are listed. Characteristically user friendly, the site allows you to "click" on the city or district you're interested in and the available resources for that location are at your fingertips. The listings give a brief description of the services as well as addresses and phone numbers.

The National Runaway Switchboard
http://www.nrscrisisline.org

Based in Chicago Illinois, the *National Runaway Switchboard* is a non-profit, volunteer organization. It operates a confidential hotline for runaway youth, teens in crisis, and concerned friends and family members. All services are free and are available 24 hours every day. Services include crisis intervention, message relay between parent and child, and referrals to community-based resources. It also operates a Home Free service in partnership with Greyhound Bus Lines to help runaways return to their families.

Royal Canadian Mounted Police Missing Children's Registry
http://www.childcybersearch.org/rcmp/

This RCMP homesite is Canada's national clearinghouse for missing children. It links all Canadian police and agencies through the *Canadian Police Information Centre* (CPIC), U.S. police agencies through the *National Crime Information Center* (NCIC), and most foreign police agencies through Interpol. Established in 1986, the Registry forms one of the most comprehensive of its kind in the world. For those wishing general information, the site provides access to an excellent library of resource materials.

Street Teams
http://www.streetteams.com

Street Teams is a unique organization based in Calgary, Alberta, Canada. Its mission is the prevention, intervention and recovery of female children who have become involved in, or are at high risk of involvement in prostitution or pornography. This web site is an excellent resource for understanding the pimp/child prostitute relationship, recruiting methods, and tactics for recovery.

Notes

CHILDREN IN THE GAME goes beyond a simple description of child prostitution by offering methods and solutions for the prevention, intervention, and reconnection of the young victims of prostitution.

With that in mind, I designed this book to be a resource book—a handbook for those called to action. These pages are left blank for you to fill as you take on the armor of awareness and contribute knowledgeably to the battle to win back the prizes in "the game"—our children.

_____

_____

_____

_____

_____

_____

_____

_____

_____

_____

_____

Testimonials

What people have said about Children in the Game...

"*Children in the Game* is a very disturbing book. The stories of children whose lives have been devastated by pimps and customers cannot help but tear at the heart and conscience of the reader.

The brutal honesty of the book is offset by the hope Ross MacInnes offers. He provides practical techniques to the many people who are fighting to save their daughters, nieces or neighbours, and he also equips the reader for the war to recover these youngsters.

This book is a 'must read' for legislators, law enforcement personnel, social workers and every adult who has a daughter, niece, or granddaughter.

It is also a must read for every teen. For they are the ones who lose the most—because a child on the street doesn't remain a child for very long.

Heather Forsyth, Member of the Alberta Legislative Assembly

"*Children in the Game* is chilling. It outlines a pattern of behaviour hardly understood and most often ignored. At its least, it is a source of understanding and potential discussion at many levels. At its best, it will achieve its objective—a call to action. Ross MacInnes' *Children in the Game* is a solid addition to the paucity of competent information on the topic of child prostitution and what can be done about the problem."

Harley Johnson, Former Ombudsman for Alberta/Yukon

"Ross MacInnes is shedding light on this ongoing criminal enterprise that has for to long been relegated to the shadows of the night. *Children in the Game* is an invaluable and long overdue guide for every parent, teen, social service worker, and member of the criminal justice system.

Ross MacInnes proves that through intervention and aftercare it is possible to stop the perpetual victimization of our youth and provide them with an opportunity for a happy, healthy life."

Detective Mike Maines, LVMP, Vice Investigation Squad, Las Vegas

"I am delighted to recommend *Children in the Game*. Ross MacInnes' work with children on the street and his commitment to *Street Teams* provides a unique insight into the world of child prostitution. It is extremely important that Ross has shared his experiences and perceptions with others in an effort to help children avoid this nightmarish lifestyle and to help adults protect the children they serve."

Dr. Lois Lee, Children of the Night Residential Program,
Los Angeles

"If you think it cannot happen in your neighborhood, think again. Predatory pimp organizations are targeting the middle class and stalking children in suburban high schools, playgrounds and shopping malls. *Children in the Game* provides a revealing look at how these pimps operate, the destruction they can cause, and what you need to do to protect your child."

Bill Kurtis, A&E Television's Investigative Reports

"Ross MacInnes certainly covers the tragic world of children caught in child prostitution in his new book *Children in the Game*. He shows the severe violence that these children must endure, their tragic childhood and the dreadful circumstances of their everyday life on the streets.

However, and perhaps most importantly, Ross also shows that these children are redeemable and can be returned to a most productive lifestyle. He shows what love can do to rehabilitate these children and the importance of awareness and education for the general public."

Frank Barnaba, President, The Paul & Lisa Street Outreach Program,
New York City

About the Author

ROSS MACINNES served as an active police officer for twenty-seven years. His final command was as head of the Calgary Police Vice Unit, where he pioneered a number of innovative programs dealing with the sexual exploitation of children.

In 1995, Ross retired from the Calgary Police Service to become the Executive Director of *Street Teams*, a non-profit agency dedicated to the prevention, intervention and recovery of female children who have become involved in prostitution or pornography or are at high risk of involvement.

He has written hundreds of articles and conference papers, and has appeared as a guest on major television network talk shows. He has lectured extensively throughout North America, including a presentation to a special mission of the United Nations.

The book *Children in the Game* reflects his experiences working with sexually exploited children. He has been married to Dee for over thirty years, and along with their two biological children have welcomed dozens of other children to their extended family over the past twenty-two years.

How does a cow do math?

With a cow-culator.

What do you get when you cross a turtle with a porcupine?

A slowpoke.

How comes lions eat raw meat?
They never learned how to cook.

What's something lazy dogs like to do for fun?
Chase cars that are parked.

Monkeys love to play football in which month?
Ape-ril.

Who's there?
Icy.
Icy who?
Icy you looking at me!

Who's there?
Alex.
Alex who?
Alex-plain later!

Why can't pirates learn the alphabet?

They keep getting lost at C.

Three tree turtles took turns talking tongue twisters. If three tree turtles took turns talking tongue twisters, where are the twisters the three tree turtles talked?

Who's there?
Harry.
Harry who?
Harry up, it's cold outside!

Who's there?
Justin.
Justin who?
Justin time for dinner.

Leave Your Feedback on Amazon

Please think about leaving some feedback via a review on Amazon. It may only take a moment, but it really does mean the world for small businesses like mine.

Even if you did not enjoy this title, please let us know the reason(s) in your review so that we may improve this title and serve you better.

From the Publisher

Hayden Fox's mission is to create premium content for children that will help them expand their vocabulary, grow their imaginations, gain confidence, and share tons of laughs along the way.

Without you, however, this would not be possible, so we sincerely thank you for your purchase and for supporting our company mission.

Check out our other books!

For more, visit our Amazon store at:
amazon.com/author/haydenfox

Made in the USA
Coppell, TX
30 November 2021

66700373R00059